Teaching About Historical

A professional resource to help teach six interrelated concepts central to students' ability to think critically about history

Authors

Mike Denos

Roland Case

Editors

Peter Seixas

Penney Clark

Series Editor

Roland Case

TC²

The Critical Thinking Consortium

Series published by

The Critical Thinking Consortium
University of British Columbia
Education Building
6365 Biological Sciences Road
Vancouver, BC Canada V6T 1Z4
Fax: 604.822.6603
Tel: 604.822.9297
e-mail: tc2@interchange.ubc.ca
www.tc2.ca

Series distributed by

Pacific Educational Press
Faculty of Education
University of British Columbia
Vancouver, BC V6T 1Z4
Tel: 604.822.5385
Fax: 604.822.6603
www.pep.educ.ubc.ca

McGraw-Hill Ryerson, School Division
300 Water Street
Whitby, ON L1N 9B6
Tel: 905.430.5247
Fax: 905.430.5023
www.mcgrawhill.ca

Cover Design: Kathie Wraight and Clarisa Niks
Interior Design: M. Kathie Wraight, Field Programs, Simon Fraser University
Production: M. Kathie Wraight, Field Programs, Simon Fraser University
Proof Reading: Emma Kendall

This publication has been supported by the **Canadian Studies Program, Canadian Heritage**. The opinions expressed do not necessarily reflect the views of the Government of Canada.

Library and Archives Canada Cataloguing in Publication

Denos, Mike, 1945-

Teaching about historical thinking : a professional resource to help teach six interrelated concepts central to students' ability to think critically about history / authors, Mike Denos, Roland Case ; editors, Peter Seixas, Penney Clark.

(Tools for historical understanding, ISSN 1910-5290)

ISBN 0-86491-286-2

1. History--Study and teaching (Secondary)--Canada. 2. Historiography--Study and teaching (Secondary)--Canada. 3. Critical thinking--Study and teaching (Secondary). I. Case, Roland, 1951- II. Seixas, Peter Carr, 1947- III. Clark, Penney, 1950- IV. Critical Thinking Consortium V. Title. VI. Series.

D16.2.D45 2006 907.1'271 C2006-905522-X

Table of Contents

Foreword

This resource is one of several publications in the *Tools for Historical Understanding* series. Our goal is to help teachers and students acquire the "tools" to think deeply and critically about history. Without these "tools," significant understanding of history is impossible.

Teaching About Historical Thinking focuses on six interrelated concepts central to students' ability to think about history. These core concepts are: historical significance, evidence, continuity and change, cause and consequence, historical perspective taking, and moral judgment. The nature and importance of each concept is discussed as are the problems associated with helping students understand them. The resource offers specific suggestions for introducing the concepts to students and for applying them throughout the history curriculum. Extended teaching examples illustrate how these concepts work in tandem as students learn to think critically about history.

This conceptual framework for historical understanding stems from the work of Peter Sexias, Professor and Canada Research Chair in Education at the University of British Columbia and Director of the Centre for the Study of Historical Consciousness. More particularly, determining what is historically *significant* is key to appreciating that judging the importance of specific facts and events in history are matters of debate and subject to change. Knowing that the past is accessed though the examination of *evidence* and learning to interpret and assess the reliability of primary and secondary sources are vital understandings for students to develop. Identifying what has changed or stayed the same over periods in history and between past and contemporary times are important questions when considering historical *continuity and change*. The concepts of *cause and consequence* help students explore the contributing influences in history. Understanding these influences makes it possible for students to see the structural and individual factors that shape their world and to begin to imagine their own role as citizens in shaping history. *Historical perspective taking* encourages students to explore how people in the past saw themselves in time and place as a means to understanding past actions in their historical contexts and not simply viewing them from the perspective of present experiences and values. The notion of *moral judgment* helps students consider the complexities of passing judgment on historical events and people and of drawing conclusions about the moral responsibility of contemporary individuals and groups in relation to past actions.

These concepts provide informed entry points or portals to think about and engage in an interpretative dialogue that lives at the heart of historical understanding.

The timing of this publication coincides with the development of "Benchmarks of Historical Thinking" by the Historica Foundation and the Centre for the Study of Historical Consciousness at the University of British Columbia. The Benchmarks project uses the same six concepts to help teachers develop classroom tasks and assessment rubrics that will measure students' advances in historical thinking over the course of the Canadian history curriculum. *Teaching About Historical Thinking* and the Benchmarks assessment tools will thus complement each other in the service of promoting a more critical Canadian history education.

Roland Case
Series editor

Introduction to historical thinking

1

The nature of historical thinking

The popular American television show *The Sopranos* is an on-going epic story about a New Jersey Mafia boss—Tony Soprano—and his family. Tony is a brutal killer when dealing with "business" matters, but he also lives an ordinary suburban life with a conventional family in New Jersey. He is a ruthless bully, but he's charming. He is merciless but he's also sensitive to the point of needing psychiatric therapy for his anxiety attacks. He's a sociopath with a close affection for his family.

An interesting episode, historically speaking, is one titled "Christopher" which takes place on a Columbus Day. One of the main themes of the episode is that a Native-American group has mounted a demonstration to disrupt the Columbus Day parade in Tony's town, and Tony's "associates"—his Italian-American gang thugs—have decided to break up the demonstration in the name of Italian pride.

A particularly relevant scene occurs in Tony Soprano's kitchen the morning of Columbus Day. Tony, his son A.J. (Anthony Junior) and Tony's wife Carmella are discussing Columbus Day. The following dialogue takes place:

Carmella: (speaking to Tony) His history teacher, Mr. Cushman, is teaching your son that if Columbus was alive today, he would go on trial for crimes against humanity, like Milosevic in, you know, Europe.

Tony: Your teacher said that?

A.J.: It's not just my teacher. It's the truth. It's in my history book!

Tony: So you finally read a book and it's bullshit.

Carmella: Tony!

Tony: Look, get into Columbus's shoes to see what he went through. People thought the world was flat for crying out loud. Then he lands on an island with a bunch of naked savages on it and it took a lot of guts. You remember when we went to Florida, the heat and those bugs?

A.J.: Like it took guts to murder people and put them in chains?

Carmella: He was a victim of his time.

A.J.: Who cares? It's what he did!

Tony: He discovered America is what he did. He was a brave Italian explorer. And in this house Christopher Columbus was a hero. End of story![1]

[1] "Christopher" Episode Three, Season 4 of *The Sopranos*.

This scene touches upon most of the kinds of issues facing historians. The characters confront the essential issues of historical thinking: What really happened? How do we know that it happened as the history books suggest? What did it feel like to be Columbus? How did it feel to be a native of Santo Domingo? Should we remember Columbus as a hero or a brute? Was Columbus' "discovery" of America really such a big event? These questions and others like them form the body of inquiry we call history.

Most high school students do not think of history with the passion shown by the Soprano family. More typically they see it as learning detailed facts of numerous past events in chronological order. Yet, whether students realize it or not, in their own lives history plays a much more vital and dynamic role, because all of us, from little children to the elderly, think about who we are and where we are in the continuum of time. And when a version of history challenges our conception of ourselves, it suddenly becomes relevant and, as Tony, Carmella and A.J. demonstrated, often crucially important to us.

Despite the fact that Tony is a mobster, A.J is a bust as a student and Carmella seems to care only about appearances, they all invested in being Italian and are concerned about how Italians are represented. Part of that perception depends on how Italians behaved in the past and how those actions are represented in contemporary historical accounts. Without much conscious thought, they are showing how present understandings and self-perceptions depend on past events and our interpretations of them.

In that short scene from The Sopranos, we see the difference between history and the past. The past is everything that has happened and can never be recounted in its totality. History is the telling of what happened and is by nature selective in that telling. In creating that narrative, by identifying what we include and exclude, and by making judgments about the merits of various actions, we make sense of the past and signal what is important to us now. The history we create depends on our present situation and purposes. Thus history, unlike the past, is never static—it changes with emerging values, ideas and audiences. *Historical thinking is the act of interpreting and assessing both the evidence from the past that has been left behind and the narratives that historians and others have constructed from this evidence.*

The importance of historical thinking

We can appreciate the importance of historical thinking by distinguishing between history as an *educational* and an *informational* subject. If history is an informational subject, its content is to be passed on by teachers and remembered by students. There is little need to question or problematize the received narratives. Teaching history as an informational subject typically means presenting an account—often framed as *the* true story of the events—which students learn and accept by absorbing the relevant factual details laid out in their textbook. In short, history becomes a body of information teachers can transmit.

This informational account of history teaching is inadequate for at least two reasons:

- students cannot properly understand history unless they know what is involved in thinking deeply and critically about it;

- students are more likely to be engaged in the study of history if they are encouarged to think critically about the subject matter.

Promoting historical understanding

Students' ability to grasp both the nature of the discipline we call history and the content they learn in history class is impaired if they do not see history as consisting of accounts that must be constructed, interpreted and assessed. In other words, neither the *subject* nor the *subject matter* of history can be properly understood without engaging in historical thinking.

The need to think critically in order to understand the discipline arises because history inevitably consists of partial accounts constructed for specific purposes. No account can present all that is known—historians must be selective in the topics they focus on and the details they mention within these topics (for example, stressing daily life over political events, famous peoples over ordinary citizens, World War I and II but not the Crimean and Korean wars). In addition, all accounts must be framed within a perspective (for example, Canadian history might be written from any number of points of views including pan-Canadian, French-Canadian, First Nations, immigrant, or American perspectives).

As new social, economic and political issues arise, we revise our perspectives on the past. Many of us were taught in school that Christopher Columbus *discovered* America; yet this is no longer the "truth." In this sense "revisionist" history is the only history there is. Though it is about the past, historical knowledge is also shaped by conditions and priorities in the present. Recently the environment, religious conflict and gender issues have acquired greater focus. Current textbooks differ in content from those in use twenty years ago and even more so than books written fifty years ago. Ten years from now, other issues will arise and our narratives and our historical understanding of the past will change with them. Unless students are taught to recognize and explore the factors that influence what gets represented as history and to understand that there can never be *the* history of an event or a period, they will not understand the nature of the subject. In this respect, history must be an educational subject.

Not only does the informational view of history teaching misrepresent the disciple, it undermines students' understanding of the subject matter. This is obviously true insofar as it is unrealistic to expect students to understand what they are learning if they misconstrue the discipline which gives rise to this knowledge. But there is an even more compelling pedagogical reason for involving students in historical thinking. Simply presenting historical facts to students typically results in this information remaining "inert," to use Alfred North Whitehead's term. By inert, Whitehead means "ideas that are merely received into the mind without being utilized, or tested, or thrown into fresh combination."[2] Students won't develop an understanding of the subject matter through passive recounting of historical details but only by thinking deeply about and with the ideas they encounter. As Walter Parker notes "Thinking is how people learn."[3] Of course students must learn the "facts" of past events, but they must think about these details and how they are selected and used to construct history.

---

[2] A.N. Whitehead. 1929/1967. *The aims of education and other essays*. New York: Free Press.

[3] W. Parker. 1989. How to help students learn history and geography. *Educational Leadership*, 47(3), 39-43.

Engaging students in the study of history

Instead of embracing history as a stimulating course, many students are bored by it. The challenge is not simply to find ways of making history more relevant to students. It's more importantly a matter of making the study of history more active. As long as students remain passive recipients of historical facts instead of inquirers into the dynamic nature of history they are less likely to be engaged. In short, involving students in thinking historically is more likely to excite students because it is inherently more appealing to be invited to think of one's own beliefs and not simply find answers that others have produced.

Dimensions of historical thinking

Peter Seixas has identified six concepts that underpin our ability to think historically. Each can be seen as a portal, as an accessible entry point to involve students in thinking critically about history. These concepts are described briefly below and elaborated upon in subsequent chapters.

Historical significance. Behind the selection of what and who should be remembered, researched, taught, and learned is the issue of historical significance. Questions of significance are foundational to thinking about history because historians cannot include all that has happened in the past and students must be concerned to learn about and appreciate the most important events. But what is important, historically speaking? How do we decide whether an historical event is significant for everybody or just for some people? Whose history is it? For Canadians, Columbus Day is not a major holiday. To Tony Soprano and the Native American people, it has major cultural and social significance. Thinking about significance helps students learn how decisions about what to report and study in history are made and to recognize that the very nature of historical inquiry is open to ongoing change.

Evidence. The concept of evidence is concerned with the validation, interpretation and use of primary and secondary sources of historical information in the construction of history and historical argument. Issues of evidence invite questions such as: How do we know what happened? Which version of events should we believe? Is this a reliable source of information? In our Sopranos' example, according to A.J., the textbook and his teacher are the sources of evidence. For Tony, the evidence is derived from his memory of what he learned in school and perhaps from his family. Their opinions are based naively upon secondary sources rooted in popular cultural. Issues of evidence invite students to scrutinize the information found in various kinds of sources, and to explore the role of primary and secondary sources in constructing accounts of the past.

Continuity and change. The concepts of continuity and change confront two historical stereotypes: either nothing really changes over time or events that occurred long ago must by definition be completely unlike modern times. The former misconception has been called "Flintstone history"—the notion that the only real difference between ourselves and people in the past is that they wore funny clothing. The latter is a form of radical relativism. Students need to investigate what has changed or stayed the same over periods in history and between past and contemporary times. Not only are the subtleties of change and continuity difficult to discern, our conceptions of each depend on life experiences and worldview. A student who has come from a country where profound change has taken place in a short period of time may view change differently than a student from a more stable environment.

Cause and consequences. The concepts of cause and consequence focus on the contributing influences in history. Understanding these influences makes it possible for students to see the structural and individual factors that shape their world and to begin to imagine their own role as citizens in shaping history. Questions of cause and consequence that the Soprano's might have but did not ask about the Columbus story include: Was Columbus primarily responsible for "discovery" of the "New World?" In what ways were events influenced by prevailing social, economic and political factors? Why did the natives of Santo Domingo not resist Columbus? Had they done so it might well have been "end of story" for Columbus. How would the events of history been altered?

Historical perspective. Entering into the perspective of historical individuals and groups requires understanding the social, cultural, intellectual, and emotional contexts that shaped people's lives and actions. Without an appreciation of how people in the past saw themselves in time and place, students will be trapped in a simplistic viewing of the past, seeing events exclusively through present experiences and values. This problem of "presentism" is apparent in the Soprano's example, when Tony equates Columbus' feelings with his own feeling towards "naked savages". Without a more sensitive understanding of the realities of another time, Tony unintentionally but mistakenly imposed his frames of reference upon the actions and beliefs of this historic figure.

Moral judgment. Moral judgments in history arise in the context of drawing ethical conclusions about historical actions and people or in assigning moral culpability to historical figures or to contemporary individuals and groups for past actions. Students must learn to consider the complexities and dangers associated with passing judgment on historical events and people. For example, Tony assumes that Columbus' "discovery" of America was a good thing. "End of story." Yet from the First Nations perspective, what was so good about the European occupation of their homeland? Should we remember Columbus as a hero or a brute? What responsibility if any might contemporary institutions and groups who have benefited from this conquest owe to descendants of First Nations people who suffered loses because of it? These are the kinds of moral judgments that students must learn to make thoughtfully and cautiously.

Inevitably as teachers we will have used these concepts periodically in our classrooms. The operative questions to ask are:

- Can we use them more frequently and systematically?
- What might we do to help students make thoughtful use of these concepts as entry points to deepening their thinking about history?

Challenges for teachers of history

Teaching about historical thinking presents challenges and will require adjustments. Below are some of the more significant ones that we may wish to embrace more completely in our teaching:

Making history problematic. We need to consistently present historical information in the context of exploring genuine inquiries where the conclusions are open for critical debate and not already prepackaged for students.

Assembling of multiple resources. Teaching historical thinking requires that students have access to a variety of primary and secondary sources that reflect a multiplicity of perspectives on the topics they explore.

Accepting alternative interpretations. We must be willing to put aside our preferred historical interpretations and welcome differing perspectives and understandings presented by students.

Using history to inform the present. We should regularly help students see that history can inform their understanding of contemporary questions and issues.

Teaching the tools. Students must understand the concepts that underpin their ability to think historically and have regular opportunities to apply these concepts as they make sense of and use the historical information they acquire.

Shifting the focus in assessment. When evaluating student work, our expectations should focus on well-justified or well thought-out explanations rather than on provision of the right answer.

In short, teaching students to think historically will require additional effort, openness, and student independence. The objective of this resource is to help teachers meet these challenges by providing practical ways to use six concepts of historical thinking as portals to deepening students' understanding of the past.

Introducing historical thinking to students

Before introducing students to specific concepts that will assist them in thinking about history, it may be useful to explore the very idea of historical thinking.

Distinguishing 'history' from 'the past'. One approach to introducing the idea of thinking historically is to distinguish between 'history' and 'the past'—history is an account of past events. The objective is to show that an historical narrative is not a static account of the truth but a constructed story based on evidence. Write the two terms on the board and invite students to identify elements that distinguish these concepts. You may want to offer examples of a past event (e.g., an accident that happened the night before) and a history of the event (e.g., a newspaper account of the accident). Eventually students will generate a list such as the one outlined below. Discuss the idea that the past is gone and only history is alive. Invite students to identify the problems in accepting history as the story of the past.

The Past	History
• The past consists of all the things that ever existed, all the words that were uttered and all the deeds done.	• History can account only for a small sampling of the past.
• The past is no longer here; it no longer exists.	• History is a way to remember the past through an organized story and analysis of the evidence of past events.
• There's no organized story to the past, but only remnants that have survived over time.	• History is influenced by a selection of aspects of the past that are considered meaningful to us in the present.

Distinguishing 'myth' and 'history'. A strategy for helping students understand that history is not simply any old story of the past is to distinguish 'myth' and 'history'. Although both are stories about the past, their purposes differ. Students may have difficulty distinguishing myths and historical accounts. To assist them in this task, read a Greek myth and an historical account of an incident in ancient Greece. Through guided questions help students generate the following comparisons.

History	Myth
• History is based on evidence.	• Myth is based on belief or faith.
• Can be challenged and changed.	• Can't challenge or change a myth.
• We want it to be challenged and revised.	• We don't want to challenge or change it.

Viewing the study of history as inquiry. For many students, the study of history is largely a matter of finding factual information on a topic—the answers already exist in textbooks. Students are simply "re-searching" the answers—locating ideas and facts that others have uncovered. Notice the term 'original research' (which may be an oxymoron) is used to indicate that a study is intended to produce new knowledge and not simply reproduce what others know already. Understood in these term, "researching" questions in history does not require historical thinking, but simply skill in information retrieval. Students need to appreciate that the study of history can be a genuine inquiry where their task is not merely to find out what others know (they must, of course, do this) but to reach a conclusion using this information. Even if others already know the answer, in a genuine inquiry students' task is to reach their own conclusions and not simply locate the conclusions offered by others. *This feature defines an inquiry question: it requires that students make a reasoned judgment about the most justifiable conclusion to reach.*

To illustrate the difference between "research" questions (involving mere factual retrieval) and inquiry questions (requiring reasoned judgment) present students with a list of parallel questions/tasks of both types as suggested below. Invite students to discuss the differences between the pairs and what is involved in answering each type. As an extension, invite students to develop their own samples of each kind of question/task.

Research questions and tasks	Inquiry questions and tasks
List five factors leading to the decision of colonies to join in Confederation.	Rank in order of importance the five identified factors leading to the decision of colonies to join in Confederation.
Describe John A. Macdonald's contributions as leader.	Was John A. Macdonald a great leader?
Compare life in New France with life in the American colonies.	What was the biggest difference between life in New France and in the American colonies.
What were the stated reasons for interning Japanese Canadians during World War II?	What were the real reasons behind the internment of Japanese Canadians during World War II?

Writing the history of an event. Inviting students to write the history of an event they have encountered is helpful in introducing the historian's role in constructing a history. Wait for an opportunity when students have witnessed an event with various elements or turns (e.g., an incident at a school assembly or in the classroom). Ask students individually to write an eye witness account of the event. Arrange for students to compare their accounts and to discuss the differences and why these might arise. Now ask students to work in groups to write a history of this event, using evidence from the various accounts. You may want to help students structure their narrative around four questions:

- What are the root causes of the incident?
- What are the key actions in the event?
- Who is responsible?
- What are its implications or consequences?

Compare the histories prepared by each group and discuss the reasons for the differing narratives.

Historical significance

2

On May 15, 1919, virtually the entire working population of Winnipeg—30,000 to 35,000 people—went on strike. The strike, which had begun two weeks earlier as a strike by the Building Trades Council and the Metal Trades Council, had grown to include firemen, postal workers, telephone operators, office clerks, transit workers, garbage collectors and many others. Even the Winnipeg police expressed support for the strike and as a result the entire force and its chief were fired and replaced. Factories, stores, restaurants—everything was shut down as workers sought recognition for their unions and the right to bargain collectively.

Business people and government responded to what they perceived as a threat to civil order. Businesses formed the "Committee of 1000" to oppose the strike. The government passed repressive laws aimed at threatening and removing the strike leaders. Armored cars, troops and machine-gun units were moved to Winnipeg.

The strike lasted six weeks and was generally peaceful. However on June 21, "Bloody Saturday," the government decided that it had had enough. During a workers' parade to protest the arrest of several strike leaders, anger exploded into riots and violence. Mounties galloped into the crowd swinging batons and firing their guns. At the end of the day, one person was dead and many were injured. The strike dissolved.

In the end, the workers gained nothing and in fact their cause was severely set back. Many lost their jobs and the union movement was, at least at that moment, stymied.

In contrast, on October 31, 1983, 35,000 members of the BC Government Employees Union went on strike to protest government legislation to cut social programs and to reduce the public service by 25 percent. A week later they were joined by almost all of the province's 30,000 school teachers. By November 13, with almost all provincial services having been shut down for almost two weeks and after several massive demonstrations, the strikers under the banner of "Operation Solidarity" were poised to be joined by 40,000 members of the International Woodworkers of America (the IWA) in a general strike. The strike was averted by a last minute meeting between Premier Bill Bennett and the president of the IWA Jack Munro at Bennett's home in Kelowna, B.C. The meeting resulted in a contentious peace package called the Kelowna Accord.

Both of these events were momentous in their times. Both had an impact on their communities and subsequent history. However, the Winnipeg General Strike is studied as a significant and major event of 20th century Canadian history in almost every history curriculum in Canada. On the other hand, "Operation Solidarity" is rarely mentioned in history curricula, even in British Columbia. Why would the Winnipeg General Strike, which accomplished nothing and in the scheme of things resulted in limited violence, be studied by all Canadians and documented in every textbook on modern Canadian history, while

Operation Solidarity, which involved many more people and had positive results for workers, is not seen as worthy of remembering even in British Columbia?

This questions raises by this example are about historical significance—*about the factors that determine what and who should be remembered, researched, taught, and learned.* These questions present some of the most fundamental and unavoidable considerations in historical thinking. The past is everything that ever happened to anyone anywhere, but we cannot remember or learn it all. Consequently we must select what to study, how to describe it and how to fit these events and trends into a larger story of the past. This requires that historians and students of history continually determine which aspects of the past are historically significant.

If students do not consider how and why certain things are selected and not others they may simply take what is presented by the textbook or the teachers to be significant, without any further thought. They may overlook the possibility that other important things may have been omitted because the person constructing the account did not judge them to be significant. Critical examination of the reasons for the inclusion and exclusion of particular events and figures is essential to students' ability to appreciate the significance and therefore the meaning of everything they study in history.

Dimensions of historical significance

The various dimensions that we might want to teach students, about the concept of historical significance and its role in historical thinking, are usefully summarized by the following principles:

Determinations of significance are unavoidable. For reasons stated above, every historical account inevitably requires leaving certain facts or questions aside and selecting others as more important. Students need to be mindful of this inevitable inclusion and exclusion and of the factors that guide these choices. Every strike in Canadian history cannot be included, and the biggest or longest strike need not be the most significant. For example, the smaller Winnipeg General Strike is judged to have greater significance than Operation Solidarity partly because of its long term impact. The earlier strike was instrumental in establishing basic workers' rights such as collective bargaining and in creating Canada's first socialist party. These developments shaped the labour and political landscape of Canada in ways that Operation Solidarity did not.

Significance depends upon one's perspective. What will be judged to be significant may vary depending upon an individual's or group's perspective. For example, the Winnipeg General Strike would be seen as more significant to a union leader than to a First Nations leader, and more significant to socialists than to environmentalists.

Significance depends upon purpose. Significance also depends on the purpose for which a question is posed. In this respect, the significance of an event depends upon its role in the larger narrative or story the historian is attempting to tell. For instance, a historian writing a women's history of Canada might not regard the Winnipeg General Strike as significant as other events of the same time, such as the "Person's Case." Similarly, biographers of J.S. Woodsworth, a leader of the Winnipeg General Strike, may judge the event's significance differently depending on whether their purpose is to chronicle the personal or public life of this individual.

Significance varies with time. The significance of an historical event may not be fixed in time but may moderate depending on subsequent events and current priorities. For instance, it may well be that the significance of the Winnipeg General Strike has lessened since the fall of the Soviet Union. Now that collective bargaining is a normal part of Canadian life, the interest in the struggle for that right might have less significance to us now that it did in the 1950's. In turn, subsequent concerns for gender equality in the workplace may supplant some of the significance attached to the Winnipeg General Strike.

Significance is not simply a matter of personal reaction. It is not sufficient when determining significance to rely exclusively on an individual's or group's felt reactions to an event. For example, it would be inadequate to claim that the Winnipeg General Strike is not significant for me because I don't know anyone who was involved in it, and I don't really care about the event. The significance of the Winnipeg General Strike for me as an individual extends well beyond my personal reactions to include the ways in which my family's working conditions, our community's standard of living and the political landscape in which we operate were altered because of that event. Although significance will be influenced by one's perspective, events that have the greatest felt effects are not necessarily the most significant. For example, a student may look upon the first day of school as her most personally significant event. Yet, other events, such as moving to a new community when the student was too young to remember, may have had more life-altering if less consciously felt implications. In assessing significance, the repercussions of events remain, whether or not the actual issues are a conscious concern to us today.

Significance depends on context. Context plays a role in determining significance: an event that is significant in one context may not be as significant in another context. This is a subtle and complex notion and is often overlooked in a history class. For example, the Black Plague and the Spanish Flu were both major events. However, in context, the Black Plague altered the course of European history far more significantly than the Spanish Flu of 1919. Likewise, the Winnipeg General Strike took place shortly after the Russian Revolution where workers forcefully took over the major cities of Russia and threatened the very foundations of capitalism. Operation Solidarity occurred at a time when there was no real threat of a communist take-over of British Columbia. The relatively greater significance of the Winnipeg strike in 1919 is dependent in part upon its historical context, particularly the aftermath of events in Russia in 1917.

Introducing the concept to students

Before expecting them to apply the concept across their study of history, it is helpful to introduce students to the idea of historical significance—what it means, the role of perspectives, and how significance might be determined.

Teaching the meaning of significance. The following activities may be used to introduce the idea of historical significance.

- ***Explore significance of personal events***. Invite students to choose four events in their own lives and explain in writing why they chose them as significant. After students have privately written about their choices, ask volunteers to share their choices with the class. As a class identify similarities in their choices and the reasons for their significance. Focus the discussion on what it means to say that an event is significant. Ask students whether an event can be significant even if they are not aware of how it has affected them.

- ***Infer significance in account***. Provide students with a passage from a textbook about a specific event and invite them to list the important aspects or facts as suggested by the text and then to identify the factors that make these aspect/facts important (e.g., affected lots of people, advanced Canadian nationhood). Alternatively, ask students to tally the frequency in which various categories of people (e.g., males and females; labourers and professionals) or events (e.g., positive and negative; military, political and social) are mentioned in a chapter or on a timeline. Analyze the results to determine the author's stance on what is historically significant during this period in history.

Exploring the role of perspectives in significance. The following activities may be used to introduce the role that perspective plays in historical significance.

- ***Compare perspectives on family history***. Ask each student to diagram the significant events in his or her family history. Arrange for students to ask another family member to privately diagram his or her choices. Invite students to compare their diagram with that of their family member to see how their histories differ. Discuss how student's choices of significance differ with their family members and what might account for these different perceptions?

- ***Develop consensus on national or global events***. Instruct students individually to identify the three most significant events of the last fifty years. You may want to provide them with a list of events to draw from. Ask students to work in groups of three or four to agree on the three most significant events among their choices. Invite each group to explain why its chosen events were most significant.

- ***Rewrite history***. Provide students with a passage from a textbook and invite them to make a list of the important aspects or facts as suggested by the text. Give them a different set of facts about this same event or suggest a different purpose for writing the account. For example, in the extended example in the back of this volume, students are asked to select two kinds of events described in Simon Fraser's diary—those that show his dependence on

First Nations people and those showing his self-reliance. Students are invited to rewrite an account of Simon Fraser's explorations in light one or the other of these two themes.

Introducing criteria for significance. The following activity is intended to introduce students to the criteria for judging historical significance.

- ***Assess personal events in light of the criteria***. Present students with a list of criteria, such as the following, for judging historical significance. Explain the categories and the range of factors within each. Invite students to identify several significant events in their own lives and to explain if and how each criterion applies. You may want to use the chart *Comparing significance* (Blackline Master #1) found at the back of this volume to structure this task. Ask students to list the events in order of significance and to explain their ranking.

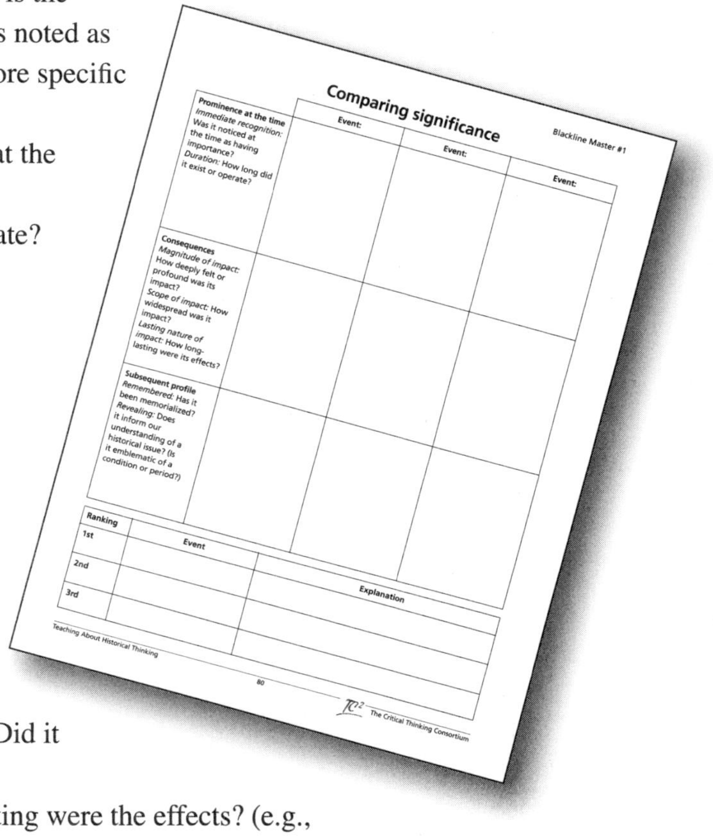

Comparing significance

Blackline Master #1

	Event:	Event:	Event:
Prominence at the time Immediate recognition: Was it noticed at the time as having importance? Duration: How long did it exist or operate?			
Consequences Magnitude of impact: How deeply felt or profound was its impact? Scope of impact: How widespread was its impact? Lasting nature of impact: How long-lasting were its effects?			
Subsequent profile Remembered: Has it been memorialized? Revealing: Does it inform our understanding of a historical issue? (Is it emblematic of a condition or period?)			

Ranking	Event	Explanation
1st		
2nd		
3rd		

Teaching About Historical Thinking 80 The Critical Thinking Consortium

  - *Prominence at the time*. One set of factors is the extent to which the event/person/trend was noted as important at the time of its occurrence. More specific criteria for judging prominence include:
    - Immediate recognition: Was it noticed at the time as having importance?
    - Duration: How long did it exist or operate?
  - *Consequences*. The most common consideration is the impact of the event/person/trend on subsequent events. More specific criteria for judging consequences include:
    - Magnitude of impact: How deeply felt or profound was the impact? (e.g., Did it result in dramatic or a minor changes?)
    - Scope of impact: How widespread was the impact? (e.g., Were many people or geographical areas affected? Did it reach across various aspects of life?)
    - Lasting nature of impact: How long lasting were the effects? (e.g., Were the effects short-lived? Did the event materially change the direction of subsequent events?)
  - *Subsequent profile*. Less widely recognized as a factor in determining significance is the importance the event/person/trend has played in popular and professional history. More specific criteria for judging the historical profile include:
    - Remembered: Has it been memorialized in popular culture or professional history? (e.g., Has it assumed iconic status within a group or society?)
    - Revealing: Does it inform our understanding of history? (e.g., Is it emblematic of a condition or period in history?)

- ***Examine the significance of popularized events.***
  Develop with students a list of notorious historical events (e.g., the Last Spike, the Alamo). Invite students to investigate whether these events deserve the historical profile they have acquired. Encourage students to suggest other related events that have less profile but may nevertheless be as significant (e.g., the workers re-enactment of the Last Spike the following day).

Applications across the curriculum

Once students have an understanding of historical significance, they are then able to employ widely this concept as a portal to thinking about historical events. Below are various ways in which it can be applied throughout the history curriculum.

Explain an event's or person's significance. Invite students to explain why a specified event or person may or may not be is significant.

> *Example*: Louis Riel's execution has become an event of considerable importance in Canadian history. Yet many rebels, especially in the United States, such as Chief Sitting Bull had been killed with as much notoriety as Louis Riel but with much less historical effect on the social conscience of the Americans. Why do we Canadians see Riel's execution as so significant?

Judge significant aspects of an event. Ask students to assess which part of an event was the most significant and why. Encourage students to consider more than the consequences but also the other criteria for historical significance.

> *Example*: In a unit on Confederation, ask students to identify the most important factor in the creation of Canada in 1867. In a debate format, ask students to offer reasons for the significance of their chosen factor and against the significance of other factors.

Compare or rank multiple events. From a list of events or historical figures, instruct students to select the most significant, or to rank order them in terms of significance.

> *Example*: Invite students to list the 5-10 early European explorers described in their textbook. Organize them to work in groups to research the significance of an assigned explorer. Arrange each group to provide a picture of its explorer and a significance rating in light of agreed upon criteria of historical significance. As each group presents its findings to the rest of the class, post the images along the board in order of their assessed significance.

Evidence

3

A popular Canadian social studies textbook[1] offers the following account of Canada's refusal to accept Jewish immigrants during the years immediately prior to World War II:

While King knew that the Nazis were persecuting Jews and other groups, he saw no need for Canada to become involved or to accept Jewish refugees. In 1938 he wrote in his diary:

> *"We must...seek to keep this part of the Continent free from unrest... Nothing can be gained by creating an internal problem in an effort to meet an international one."*

Canada's Secretary of State, Pierre Rinfret, had other reasons for rejecting Jewish refugees. In 1939, he told a meeting of his supporters that, "despite all sentiments of humanity, so long as Canada has an unemployment problem, there will be no 'open door' policy to political refugees here."

After the Krstallnacht incident, Thomas Crerar, who was now a Liberal cabinet member, made a recommendation that 10,000 Jews be allowed to emigrate to Canada. The Cabinet refused Crerar's suggestion. Immigration director Fred Blair was against Jews coming to Canada, maintaining that "none is too many." Canada's policy had tragic consequences in 1939 when the ocean liner the St. Louis, with over 900 Jewish refugees on board was refused permission to dock when it appeared off the east coast of Canada. The ship was forced to return to Europe, where many of the passengers later died in concentration camps.

Many Canadians did not share the government's anti-Semitic views. In 1938 there were 165,000 Jewish people living in Canada, the vast majority of whom were citizens. Rallies were held in many parts of the country in support of a more humane immigration policy. When the St. Louis was turned away, and its passengers sent back to Nazi Germany, newspaper editorials also lashed out at the government:

> *"The country still has the bars up and the refugee who gets into Canada has to pass some mighty stiff obstacles—deliberately placed there by the government...Immigration bars...are undesirable...We are deliberately keeping out of this country [people] and money who would greatly add to our productive revenues. We are cutting off our nose to spite our face."*

Source: Winnipeg Free Press, July 19, 1939

This account suggests that most but not all members of the Cabinet and a senior civil servant were against Jewish immigration for varying social, economic and racial reasons; while many ordinary citizens and newspaper editors were critical of the government's policy. The evidence offered in support of these conclusions are edited excerpts from various primary sources and reported accounts of the actions of selected individuals and groups.

---

1 M. Cranny and G. Moles. 2001. *Counterpoints,* Scarborough, ON: Prentice Hall, pp. 97-98

Does this account of official and popular sentiments regarding Jewish immigration accurately represent the times? Have the textbook authors provided adequate support for their conclusions? What, if anything, can we do to help students answer these two questions for themselves? The issues raised by all three questions focus on evidence. By evidence we mean: *the validation, interpretation and use of primary and secondary sources of historical information in the construction of historical accounts and arguments.*

The need to critically examine evidence is self-evident to anyone who has studied history. It is the basis of all historical understanding and unavoidable in any discussion about history. Understanding the sources and limitations of historical evidence is necessary if students are to appreciate the tentative nature of historical knowledge.

Learning about primary sources of information helps student understand that history is not simply a description of "what happened." We cannot know what happened unless we learn about it through sources that have been left behind and discovered, be they artifacts (e.g., tools, photographs, buildings, drawings), documents (e.g., wills, catalogues, posters) or written and oral descriptions.

Learning about secondary sources of information, with all of their limitations, enables students to approach textbooks and other historical accounts with a critical eye—viewing them not as "the truth" about the past but as one perspective that may or may not be justifiable given the available historical record.

Dimensions of evidence

The various aspects that are the foundation for student understanding of historical evidence are usefully summarized by the following principles:

Historical evidence is not the same as historical information. Evidence is information offered to establish a fact or point in question. This means any particular piece of information about the past becomes evidence only in response to an historical theory, issue or problem. If students are simply recalling facts about the past they are not dealing with historical evidence. Information becomes evidence occurs only if students are asked to offer reasoned arguments, reach warranted conclusions or construct plausible accounts. On its own, the fact that a bureaucrat may have said "None is too many" is simply historical information. This statement becomes evidence when it is used as an argument supporting the theory that unlike ordinary citizens, the Canadian government was not welcoming of Jewish immigrants.

Evidence is derived from two sources of information. Evidence can be found in primary and secondary sources. *A source is primary if it is original or first-hand in terms of time and access to the event. A secondary source is a one that has been constructed from other sources of information—it is second-hand; it is not direct in its access to the past.* Primary sources can be natural records (e.g., rings of a tree, fossils, volcanic ash, soil samples) or constructed artifacts and documents (e.g., child's toys, train schedules, population census, newspaper ads, diaries, or sketches of the day's events) that are from or close to the time under study. Secondary sources include deliberately prepared accounts (e.g., narratives by historians, history textbooks, second-hand reports, movies about the past) and created artifacts (e.g., replicas of lost historical objects, translations of obscure documents, reconstructed scenes in a living museum) that are produced from information drawn from other sources. A beginning step in examining the conclusions offered by the textbook account of Canada's treatment of Jewish refugees is for students to recognize that this is a secondary account which draws upon both primary and secondary sources of information.

Primary sources are our connections to the past. Primary sources are the "raw materials" upon which our historical conclusions are based. Although students will rely extensively on secondary accounts as their sources of historical information, they need to appreciate that these accounts are dependent upon and only as good as the primary sources upon which they are based. The surviving primary record offers glimpses only and typically uneven glimpses into a given historical event or period. When examining the textbook account, we would want students to appreciate that the authors' claims about Canadians' attitudes towards Jewish refugees depend ultimately on the primary sources that have been left behind. We might also want to point out that most high school textbooks rely overwhelmingly on secondary sources, so that the information and interpretations are often second- or third-hand.

Information can be drawn from traces or accounts of the past. Secondary or primary sources can provide accounts or traces of the past.

- *Accounts* describe, explain or "account for" an event. They are a deliberate telling or reckoning of the event or period. An account can be a primary (or first-hand) source of information (e.g., a eyewitness report, trial transcripts) or a secondary (or second-hand) source (e.g., a history textbook, documentary).
- *Traces* are simply remnants of the past—marks, documents or other artifacts left behind that might offer clues about an event or period. A trace is generally understood to be a primary source of information (e.g., photograph, ticket stub, legal will). However, traces can be reconstructed or simulated (e.g., a staged photograph taken years after the event, replica of a lost original object created by consulting available records). A "reconstructed" trace is a secondary source because it is not actually a remnant of the past but a recreation of the remnant based on other sources.

Traces can be sources of surprisingly varied pieces of historical information. For example, historic photographs offer us much more than information about their subjects, but also clues as to the materials used in photography of the time, glimpses of the photographic style of the period, and insights into the photographer's personal and professional tastes. Even reconstructed traces (e.g., simulations of Egyptian pyramid-building technology, the Trojan horse, ancient seafaring technology) can provide useful information about the past. Edward C. Curtis, who photographed First Nations communities at the turn of the 20th century, wanted to preserve a record of their vanishing cultures. He sometimes created his own historical evidence by arranging for people to don traditional clothing he had brought with him.

Accounts can be used as sources of information unintended by the author and in this respect these documents serve as traces—they cease to be used as deliberate reckonings but are used to offer clues about other aspects of the past. For example, a 1920's high school textbook on Canadian history can be seen as a secondary account of our national history, but it may also offer traces of textbook writers' conceptions of Canadian history, of the reading ability of secondary students, and of the quality of textbook publishing in the 1920s. Similarly, a personal diary or other primary account can offer trace evidence of things not intentionally recounted by the author (e.g., the writer's choice of language provides clues as to the linguistic customs of the period). To make the point in different words, secondary or primary accounts can also be used as primary traces, depending on the question being asked of them.

The textbook reference to a newspaper editorial lashing out at the government's immigration policy is a primary account by the editors of their views on the issue and is used as trace evidence (especially since there were similar editorials written in newspapers across the country) to support an impression of significant popular support for accepting Jewish refugees into Canada.

The validity of evidence depends on its source and use. The reason for distinguishing the differing sources (primary or secondary) and uses (as traces or accounts) of evidence is that the criteria for assessing validity will vary. As the following chart outlines, primary traces are assessed for *authenticity*, whereas secondary (reconstructed) traces are assessed for *realism;* primary accounts are assessed for *credibility* and secondary accounts for *justifiability*.

	Trace (or clue) including a "reconstructed" trace	**Account (or deliberate reckoning) of the past**
Primary source	***Authentic:*** Is the item actually what it purports to be? (e.g., Is it a genuine artefact or has it been forged or altered? Was it actually produced at the time by the identified creator?)	***Credible:*** Has the author provided a full and faithful report of what was seen, heard, said, and felt? (e.g., Was she present at the time? What social and contextual factors might influence what she reports?)
Secondary source	***Realistic:*** Does the item faithfully recreate the original document or object? (e.g., Is it a close likeness? Are the choices made plausible given the available historical record?)	***Justifiable:*** Are the conclusions in the account justifiable? (e.g., Are the sources of information reliable? Are relevant facts offered? Is there adequate evidence to draw these proffered conclusions? Is there other information that might support a different conclusion?)

Let us look at the implications of these varying criteria for students' assessment of the textbook account of Canada's immigration policy in the 1930s. Students might begin with the authenticity and credibility of the primary sources. For example, the authors cite an excerpt from King's diary as evidence of the Prime Minister's reasons for opposing Jewish immigration. While we might judge King's diary to be a credible account of his personal views, the authors omitted part of King's entry on this subject. When the missing clause is read, the passage supports a racially motivated justification for King's actions ("We must...seek to keep this part of the Continent free from unrest *and from too great an intermixture of foreign strains of blood*). This puts a different slant on the textbook authors' attributed motive of preserving social harmony.

The textbook authors attribute the quote "none is too many" to Immigration director Fred Blair. In the book, *None Is Too Many,*[2] the quote is attributed to an anonymous senior official. The textbook seemingly identifies the discriminatory policy as the work of Blair, but the quote and the underlying attitude may have been voiced by others. The uncertain source of the quote leaves the textbook without any reported evidence of Blair's attitudes.

The reported evidence of ordinary Canadians' sympathies for the plight of the Jews consists of the claim that "rallies were held in many parts of the country" and many editorials criticized the government's refusal to accept the refugees on the *S.S. St. Louis*. How adequately does this evidence justify the authors' conclusions? The reference to rallies is a vague indicator of Canadian attitudes. It would matter whether the rallies were attended by hordes or by handfuls. A more balanced account might mention evidence suggesting a lack of Canadian support for the refugees. For example, in 1939 Quebec M.P. Wilfred Lacroix delivered a petition with 127,364 signatures to the House of Common on behalf of La Société St-Jean-Baptiste "vigorously protesting against all immigration whatsoever and especially Jewish immigration*"*[3] Also, it would have been instructive to compare the number of anti-government editorials with the number supporting the government's position.

Based on the above analysis, students might be left with several conclusions about the justifiability of the textbook account:

- some of the primary evidence provided by the authors is incomplete, potentially misleading and possibly wrongly attributed;
- King's motives may have been more racially biased than the account suggests;
- the conclusions about Canadian attitudes towards Jewish immigration are supported with ambiguous and one-sided evidence.

---

[2] I. Abella and H Troper. *1997. None is too many: Canada and the Jews of Europe 1933-1948* Toronto: Lester Publishing.

[3] Petition, *House of Commons Debates,* Monday, January 30, 1939.

Introducing the concept to students

Before examining evidence in various aspects of their study of history, it is useful to introduce students to the types and uses of evidence, and to criteria for assessing the validity of evidence.

Explaining the sources and uses of evidence. The following activities may help students recognize the different sources and uses of evidence.

- ***Distinguish primary and secondary sources.*** Inviting students to distinguish primary from secondary sources is a common teaching activity. Often it is taught in an oversimplified manner by asking students to classify an identified document as *either* a primary or secondary source. However, as discussed above, a secondary source (e.g., history textbook) can be a primary source of information if used in a manner unintended by the author (e.g., providing evidence of textbook authors' attitudes). Instead, present students with an historical question (e.g., Were 1950s high school students good readers?) and suggest several possible sources (e.g., a teacher's diary describing a reading lesson in the1950s, a 1950s high school textbook written by a university professor, a history of students' reading performance over the last one hundred years). Ask students to explain what kind of source each is (primary or secondary) and identify which source might provide the most useful evidence to answer this question. You might then present a different question (e.g., What topics were studied in schools during the1950s?). Using the same documents, ask students to classify the type and relevance of each source.

- ***Analyze a simple historical artefact.*** Traces or remnants do not tell a story, but in their own way they contain information about the past. Select a simple historical trace, preferably an artefact that students can physically examine (e.g., an original photograph, tool, old book). Begin with the following questions:
  - *Who* is in the image or who would use the object?
  - *What* are the people in the image doing or what is the object?
  - *Where* does the action take place or where would the object be used?
  - *When* does the action take place or when would the object be used?
  - *Why* are the people doing this or why would the object be used? (What is its function?)
  - *How* did the people come to this situation or how was the object created and used?

  Now ask students to think about the 'traces" of information this artefact might supply about the past. You may want to prompt students with the following kinds of questions:
  - What questions about the past might this object help us answer? (e.g., Can the object tell us if the community was prosperous or poor? well-educated or illiterate? urban or rural?)
  - For each question, what answers can we draw from this source and what evidence supports these conclusions?

Ask students to record their ideas, perhaps using the chart *Analyzing traces* (Blackline Master #2) found at the back of this volume.

- ***Construct an historical account.*** The ultimate purpose in exploring evidence is to help students appreciate the challenges that historians face as they construct accounts relying largely on primary sources. Assemble a box of various documents (e.g., photographs of family, home and memorable events; report cards; pages from high school yearbook; sample writings) from your own adolescent life or that of a person unknown to students. Ask students to construct an account of the life of the featured individual looking to offer insights into the time and the person's inner life. Prior to writing the account suggest that students create a detailed list of all the claims they can make about the person and the evidence to support each claim:
  - *claim*: the person lived in Ottawa;
  - *evidence*: her picture appears in the Ottawa Regional High School yearbook.

  Encourage students to consult other sources to supplement the supplied sources. Arrange for students to share their completed accounts and the evidence for their claims. Provide students with the actual details of the featured person's life and discuss the difficulties and limitations in constructing historical accounts.

Assessing the validity of evidence. The following activities may help students learn to assess the credibility of primary accounts and the justifiability of secondary accounts.

- ***Assess the credibility of an eyewitness account.*** Explain to students that many primary sources are eyewitness accounts—that is, accounts prepared at or close to the time of the event by someone who directly experienced it. Present students with an eyewitness account of an actual or fictional incident that occurred at school (e.g., a student reporting on how her homework was lost when she tried to chase away a dog who was threatening a young child). Ask them to assess the credibility of this account using the criteria listed below. Embed into the account clues that will allow students to form hypotheses about how well each of these criteria are met. You may want students to complete the chart *Judging the credibility of primary accounts* (Blackline Master #3) found at the back of this volume.

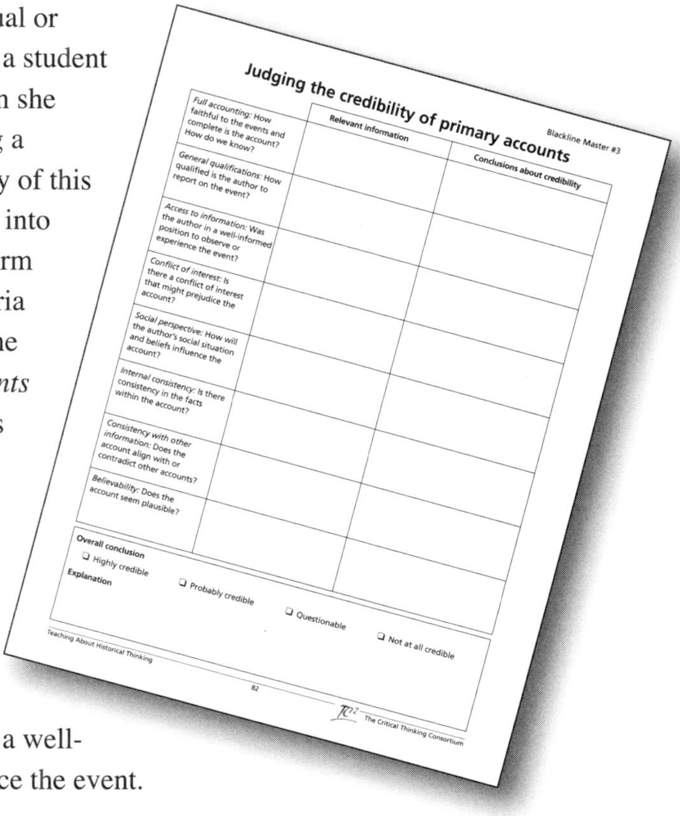
Blackline Master #3

Judging the credibility of primary accounts

	Relevant information	Conclusions about credibility
Full accounting: How faithful to the events and complete is the account? How do we know?		
General qualifications: How qualified is the author to report on the event?		
Access to information: Was the author in a well-informed position to observe or experience the event?		
Conflict of interest: Is there a conflict of interest that might prejudice the account?		
Social perspective: How will the author's social situation and beliefs influence the account?		
Internal consistency: Is there consistency in the facts within the account?		
Consistency with other information: Does the account align with or contradict other accounts?		
Believability: Does the account seem plausible?		

Overall conclusion
❑ Highly credible ❑ Probably credible ❑ Questionable ❑ Not at all credible

Explanation

Teaching About Historical Thinking 82 The Critical Thinking Consortium

  - *Full accounting:* How faithful to the events and complete is the account? How do we know?
  - *General qualifications*: How qualified is the author to report on the event?
  - *Access to information*: Was the author in a well-informed position to observe or experience the event.

- *Conflict of interest*: Is there an obvious conflict of interest that might prejudice the account?
- *Social perspective*: How will the author's social situation and beliefs influence the telling?
- *Internal consistency*: Is there a consistency in the facts within the account?
- *Consistency with other information*: Does the account align with or contradict other accounts?
- *Believability*: Does the account seem plausible?

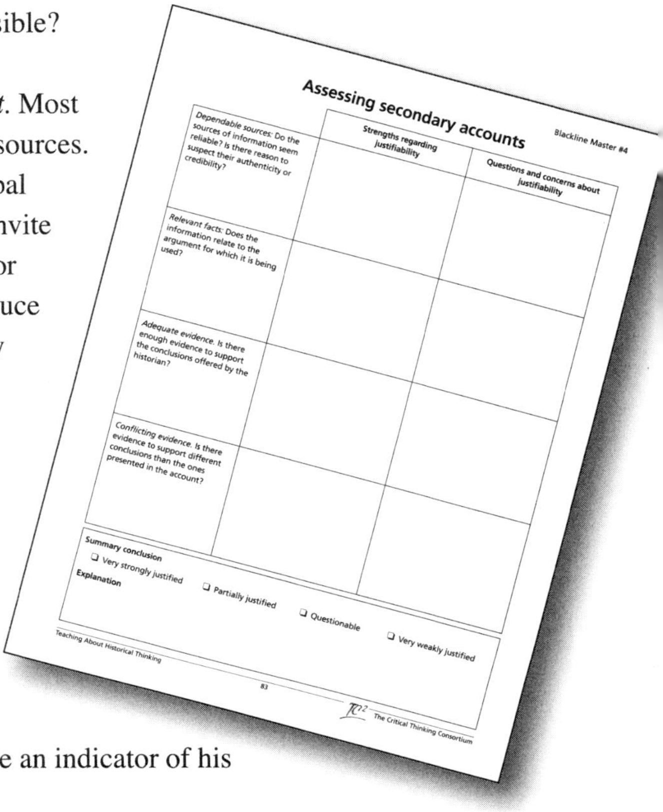

Assessing secondary accounts

Blackline Master #4

	Strengths regarding justifiability	Questions and concerns about justifiability
Dependable sources: Do the sources of information seem reliable? Is there reason to suspect their authenticity or credibility?		
Relevant facts: Does the information relate to the argument for which it is being used?		
Adequate evidence. Is there enough evidence to support the conclusions offered by the historian?		
Conflicting evidence. Is there evidence to support different conclusions than the ones presented in the account?		

Summary conclusion

❑ Very strongly justified ❑ Partially justified ❑ Questionable ❑ Very weakly justified

Explanation

Teaching About Historical Thinking 83 TC² The Critical Thinking Consortium

- ***Assess the justifiability of a newspaper account.*** Most accounts that students encounter are secondary sources. Select a newspaper account of a national or global event that offers a conclusion about the event. Invite students to indicate whether they think the author has justified the conclusion offered. Then introduce students to the criteria for assessing justifiability listed below. Provide an additional newspaper article that interprets the event differently. Ask students to asses the original article by completing the chart *Assessing secondary accounts* (Blackline Master #4) found at the back of this volume.
  - *Dependable sources:* Do the sources of information seem reliable. Is there reason to suspect their authenticity or credibility? (e.g., Is King's diary as reliable an indicator of his views as a speech made in public?)
  - *Relevant facts*: Does the information relate to the argument for which it is being used? (e.g., In trying to decide about ordinary citizens' views, is it relevant what newspaper editorials written at the time were saying?)
  - *Adequate evidence*: Is there enough evidence to support the conclusions offered by the historian (e.g., Do several public demonstrations establish that prevailing attitudes at the time were supportive of Jewish immigration?)
  - *Conflicting evidence*: Is there evidence to support a different conclusion than the one presented in the account? (e.g., Is there conflicting evidence about Canadians' support for Jewish immigration?)

Applications across the curriculum

Once students have an understanding of evidence and how it can be used and assessed, they can then apply this concept throughout the history curriculum in the following ways.

Examine visual traces in the textbook. Textbooks are filled with graphics and other visual traces that are often ignored as decoration. Regularly invite students to examine these images. Encourage students to identify and answer questions about the period that might be illuminated by these visual traces.

> *Example*: Ask students to examine WWII recruitment and propaganda posters, such as those reproduced below. Using the chart *Analyzing traces* (Blackline Master #2) ask students to study the posters and answer the "5Ws and How" questions. After sharing their conclusions and supporting evidence, direct students' attention to questions that these posters might help us answer about this period. You may want to suggest the following:
>
> - What profile of person (e.g., age, gender, social class, ethnicity) was wanted in the air force?
> - What emotions were used to motivate people during the war?
> - Did these propaganda and recruitment efforts target women, men or both?

Compare primary accounts. Present students with two or more eyewitness accounts describing the same event from differing perspectives. Invite them to assess the relatively credibility of the documents. You may want students to use the chart *Judging the credibility of primary accounts* (Blackline Master #3).

> *Example*: Locate transcripts from the trial of Louis Riel and provide students with several eyewitness accounts (e.g., testimony from both prosecution and defence witnesses). Ask students to decide which testimony is most credible.

Assess textbook accounts. Regularly invite students to consider the degree to which their textbook accounts are justifiable. Select a textbook passage such as the one used at the start of this chapter. Prepare a background sheet that provides context for the event and includes supplemental information from primary and secondary sources that challenges and confirms evidence offered in the account. Alternatively, provide an additional secondary source, such as an account from another textbook, which interprets the event differently. Ask students to assess the original account by completing the chart *Assessing secondary accounts* (Blackline Master #4).

> *Example*: Present students with the following two accounts of the building of the Canadian Pacific Railway. Ask students to contrast the two accounts (e.g., the different objectives suggested, the reasonableness of Macdonald's dream). Invite students to decide which account is historically more justifiable.

The Dream of a Railway
John A. Macdonald had a dream to link Canada's east and west coasts with a ribbon of steel. British Columbia had joined Canada on the promise that a railway would be built. But a railway had other advantages as well. It would encourage westward expansion and settlement by moving settlers west and bringing their farm products to eastern markets. But what a task a transcontinental railway was! Surveyors were required to find the best route through swamps, forests, mountains and plains. Expert engineers were needed to build bridges and blast tunnels. Thousands of labourers would have to perform the back breaking work of putting down track. But above all else, it would cost a lot of money.[4]

The National Dream
. . . British Columbia entered Confederation in 1871 with the promise of a transcontinental railroad link to the rest of Canada within ten years. At the time, this promise seemed extravagant if not rash. No politician had a clear idea of the route the railroad would follow, nor did they know how much a railroad would cost. It is conceivable that if Macdonald had known the final cost of building the railroad or the problems it would entail, he might never have made such a promise to British Columbia.

[4] J.B. Cruxton and W.D. Wilson. 1997. *Challenge of the West,* Toronto: Oxford University Press, pp. 113-114.

Macdonald had a dream of creating a British North American nation that would rival the United States. He understood correctly that the only way to realize the dream was to build a transportation and communication link that would join all the parts of British North America. Macdonald also knew that the railroad had to be built quickly. Otherwise, Canada ran the risk of being assimilated by the United States.[5]

Develop an historical argument. Students must learn to use multiple primary and secondary sources when assembling evidence to make an historical argument. The essay questions from the Bebgie Contest provide excellent sets of documents for this purpose. (In the Begbie Contest, students must draw upon short excerpts from ten text and visual documents to justify their position on an assigned issue.) To help students analyze the various sources and reach their conclusion, introduce the guidelines described in *Using multiple historical sources* (Blackline Master #5) and the chart *Document analysis* (Blackline Master #6) found at the back of this volume.

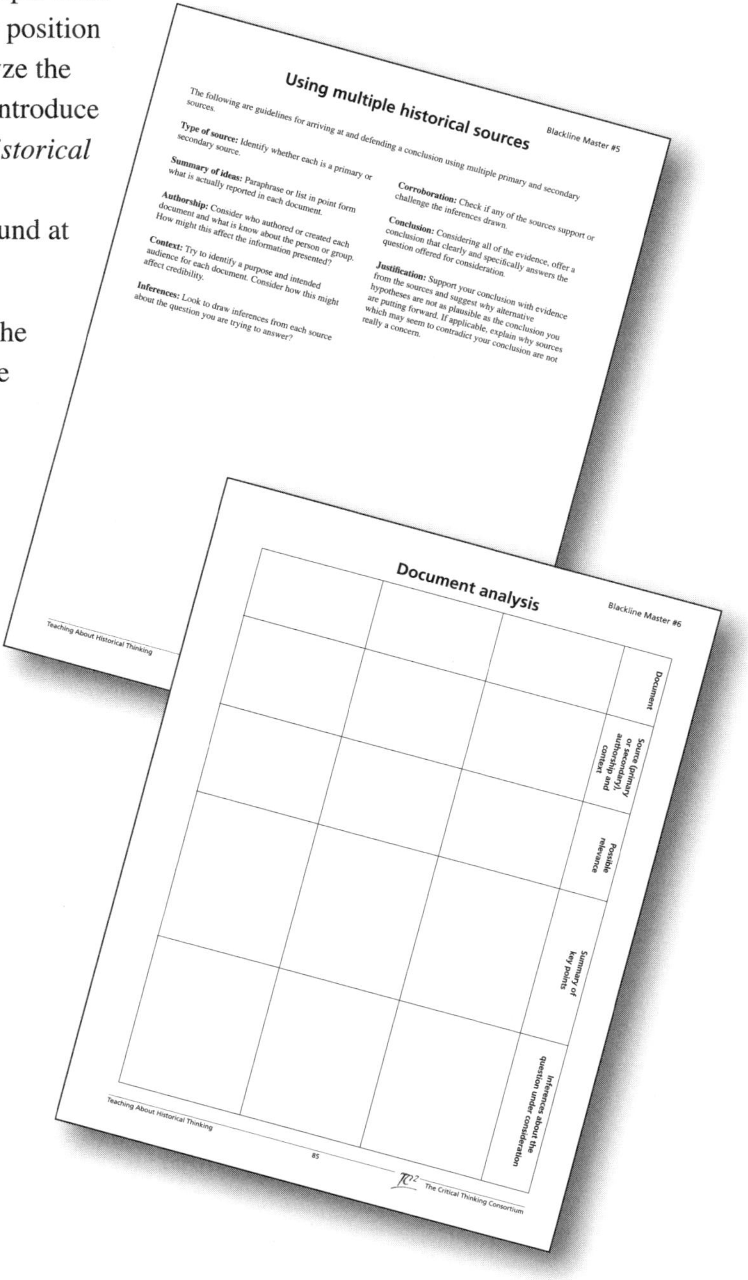

Example: Using documents found in the 2005 Begbie Contest booklet[6], provide students with the advertisements, editorial cartoons and excerpts from newspaper articles on changing patterns in male and female bathing suits. Ask students to prepare a short essay explaining why the "sun tan" bathing suit in the 1930s was controversial.

[4] M. Cranny, Jarvis, G. Moles, and B. Seney. 1999. *Horizons: Canada Moves West*. Scarborough, ON: Prentice Hall. p. 183.

[6] Available from The Begbie Contest Society, 3738 West 39th Ave, Vancouver, BC V6N 3A2 (phone: 604-266-2214).

Continuity and change

4

The following pictures depict houses in Vancouver spanning a number of decades. Arrange them in chronological sequence and, if you can, suggest an approximate decade for each picture. Note the details in the photographs that help to sequence them—features that are common to some of the houses and features that are distinct.

Photo A
(Charles S. Bailey photo,
City of Vancouver Archives SGN 1035)

Photo D
(City of Vancouver Archives CVA 1399-42)

Photo B
(Stuart Thomson photo,
City of Vancouver Archives CVA 99-1347)

Photo E
(M. Denos photo)

Photo C
(Stuart Thomson photo,
City of Vancouver Archives CVA 99-1363)

The houses in the pictures span approximately one hundred years (from the 1890s to 1994). Some are easier to place and others are more difficult. Here are the answers:

A.	189?	Family standing in front of house, Vancouver
B.	ca 1920	House in Kitsilano
C.	1920	House at 1846 15th Avenue West built under soldiers' housing scheme
D.	1947	Culter residence, 5781 Newton Wynd, University Endowment Lands
E.	1994	Westside Vancouver house

The focus of this comparison of housing styles is continuity and change. The old expression "the more things change, the more they remain the same" is of course only partially true. It may be more accurate to state that while everything has changed in certain respects, in other aspects they remain constant. This conclusion can be seen in the photographs presented above.

What is most apparent is that the houses are often more similar than they are different. All of the houses share common features no matter when they were built. They are all wood structures. They all have windows, doors, roofs, and street access. What might really make them different is what is inside of them. Some would be lit be candle light, some by gas light and some by electricity. Some would have warm and cold running water and bathrooms, and others would have outhouses and water pumps. It is interesting to speculate on the different amenities that each house might feature. There are some noticeable differences, but they do not necessarily follow an obvious pattern. The Vancouver house built in 1994 (photo E) looks more like the house of the 1920's (photo B) than the Vancouver house of 1947 (photo D). Conversely, the two houses built in the 1920s (photos B and C) look very different, even though they originate in the same decade and city. What might we consider to be the biggest changes in the houses over the 100 years?

The concepts of continuity and change are *the basis for exploring how lives and conditions are alike over periods of time and how they changed from the people and societies that come before or after*. Learning to identify significant changes as well as the constants of human existence helps us to understand our place in the continuum of time. To a large extent our references points in history are anchored in how we have changed from previous times and how we are alike (e.g., the industrial revolution, pre- and post-computers, the nuclear age, the information age).

Dimensions of continuity and change

The foundations of students' understanding of historical continuity and change are usefully summarized by the following principles:

Change and continuity are ongoing and ever present. In every aspect of our lives, things are changing and in other respects they remain constant. The form of houses and much of the building materials used in houses in North America have remained fairly constant over the last century. In the photographs of Vancouver houses, it is interesting that the 1994 "craftsman" house is a deliberate copy of an earlier popular style. In many other respects—heating, plumbing and sewage, appliances, insulating materials and fire retardants—housing has changed dramatically and with them the way we live.

Change can occur at different rates. Change can occur at a slow evolutionary pace that is almost imperceptible or it can come about dramatically and suddenly. Dramatic changes are often associated with turning points in history. In this respect, continuity and change are fundamentally linked. Understanding the rate of change depends on assumptions of continuity. For example, the Vancouver houses are general similar from the 1890s to the 1940s, but in 1947 something dramatic occurred architecturally to create a noticeably different style of house.

Change and continuity can be both positive and negative. Change does not necessarily imply progress nor does continuity necessarily imply stagnation. The assumption underlying many textbooks is one of progress and many students seem to believe if something is new it must be better. It is easy to see why such a notion would dominate. For most people in North America, things have improved, at least materially. And yet there are things that have worsened (e.g., pollution, world hunger, AIDS, drug addiction). The purpose in distinguishing change from improvement is to discourage students from making simplistic judgments about the value or desirability of similarities and differences in history. For example, while the comfort level offered by the Vancouver houses may have improved over the years, the environment around those houses may have degraded in terms of traffic, pollution and crime. While the exterior of the houses remain fairly similar, the comfort level in the newer ones would have been unattainable in the older ones. On the other hand, the house of 1890 was not subject to electrical blackouts. A fire would keep the house warm and a wood stove would cook the food, snowstorm or not.

Comparisons can be made between points in history and between the past and the present. Historical change and continuity make sense across three kinds of comparisons:

- between and among co-existing historical events, people or places (e.g., How did daily life in 1920's rural Alberta differ from urban life at that time in Montreal?);
- between and among historical periods (e.g., Was life in a 1920's bungalow substantially different from living in a Victorian house of 1890?);
- between contemporary society and earlier times (e.g., How is housing different now compared to 50 years ago?).

Periodization is a way of marking historical change and continuity. Historical periods or eras are defined by continuity in at least one dominant aspect (e.g., the Roaring Twenties, the Great Depression, the Computer Age). The arrival of a new era heralds a significant element of change in at least one 'defining' respect. For example, Vancouver houses of the 1890's reflect the Victorian style of detailed decoration while the house of 1947 represents a modern style of clean lines and glass. One is meant to display warmth and the other functionality. Of course, changes are not always abrupt; there is much continuity in other respects between historical periods (e.g., building materials, use of windows, shapes of roofs) and there are great changes in many respects within a period (e.g., advent of electricity, changing economic conditions). In this respect, identification of historical periods depend on the issues that concern us most. A focus on different dimensions of comparison would alter dramatically the periodization of history. For example, if we used entertainment technology (instead of the Great Wars) to mark the course of 20th Century Canadian history, then key periods might include the age of radio, of television, of computers, and of iPods.

Introducing the concepts to students

Before applying these concepts in various aspects of their study of history, it is worthwhile helping students recognize the pervasiveness of historical change and continuity and see the positive and negative implications of change.

Recognizing the pervasiveness of change and continuity. The following activities may be used to introduce the pervasiveness of historical change and continuity.

- ***Imagine a different time.*** Introduce the topic of change and continuity by presenting students with a list of common objects and customs (e.g., toothpaste, church weddings, hockey teams, pens) and ask them to indicate whether or not these were present at an earlier point in history. The activity *Then and now* (Blackline Master #7)[1] found at the back of this volume invites students to determine which objects and customs, from a list of 100 common items, existed two hundred years ago in Canada. Ask students to research items they are not sure of and discuss the lifestyle of people living with or without these items.

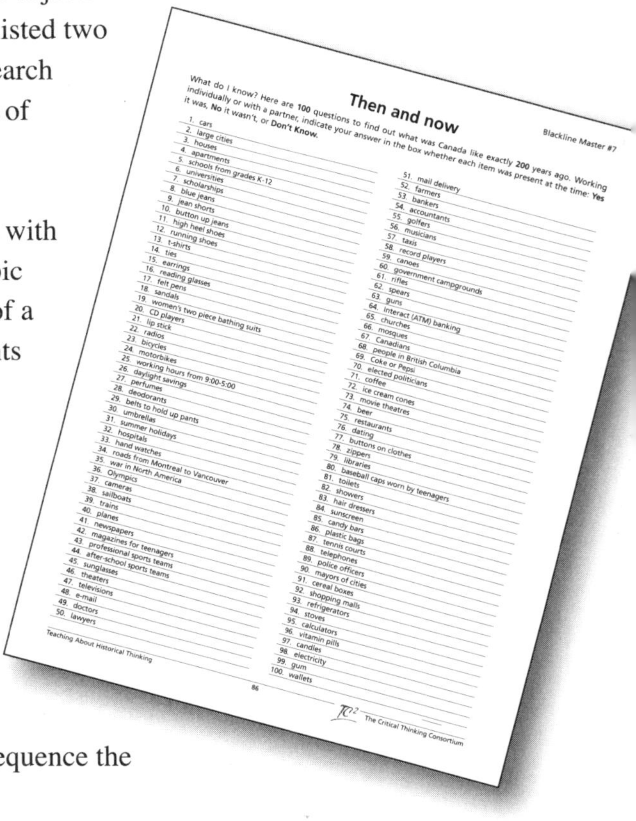

Then and now

Blackline Master #7

What do I know? Here are 100 questions to find out what was Canada like exactly 200 years ago. Working individually or with a partner, indicate your answer in the box whether each item was present at the time: Yes it was, No it wasn't, or Don't Know.

1. cars
2. large cities
3. houses
4. apartments
5. schools from grades K-12
6. universities
7. scholarships
8. blue jeans
9. jean shorts
10. button up jeans
11. high heel shoes
12. running shoes
13. t-shirts
14. ties
15. earrings
16. reading glasses
17. felt pens
18. sandals
19. women's two piece bathing suits
20. CD players
21. lip stick
22. radios
23. bicycles
24. motorbikes
25. working hours from 9:00-5:00
26. daylight savings
27. perfumes
28. deodorants
29. belts to hold up pants
30. umbrellas
31. summer holidays
32. hospitals
33. hand watches
34. roads from Montreal to Vancouver
35. war in North America
36. Olympics
37. cameras
38. sailboats
39. trains
40. planes
41. newspapers
42. magazines for teenagers
43. professional sports teams
44. after-school sports teams
45. sunglasses
46. theaters
47. televisions
48. e-mail
49. doctors
50. lawyers
51. mail delivery
52. farmers
53. bankers
54. accountants
55. golfers
56. musicians
57. taxis
58. record players
59. canoes
60. government campgrounds
61. rifles
62. spears
63. guns
64. Interact (ATM) banking
65. churches
66. mosques
67. Canadians
68. people in British Columbia
69. Coke or Pepsi
70. elected politicians
71. coffee
72. ice cream cones
73. movie theatres
74. beer
75. restaurants
76. dating
77. buttons on clothes
78. zippers
79. libraries
80. baseball caps worn by teenagers
81. toilets
82. showers
83. hair dressers
84. sunscreen
85. candy bars
86. plastic bags
87. tennis courts
88. telephones
89. police officers
90. mayors of cities
91. cereal boxes
92. shopping malls
93. refrigerators
94. stoves
95. calculators
96. vitamin pills
97. candles
98. electricity
99. gum
100. wallets

Teaching About Historical Thinking 86 The Critical Thinking Consortium

- ***Sequence images or documents.*** Present students with a series of images or documents on a common topic over several decades or periods (e.g., the history of a Canadian city over the last 100 years). Ask students to place the images/documents in chronological order, explaining their reasons. Several web sites have excellent comparative photo archives. The McCord Museum in Montreal has an outstanding website[2] comparing the same area of Montreal at different times. See the Library and Archives of Canada[3] and the City of Vancouver Archives[4] for collections suitable for this purpose. Ask students to note the clues (both what has changed and what has remained the same) that helped to sequence the images/documents.

---

[1] This activity was developed by Patricio Gonzoles.
[2] See Urban Life Through 2 Lenses www.mccord-museum.qc.ca
[3] http://www.collectionscanada.ca/index-e.html
[4] www.city.vancouver.bc.ca/ctyclerk/archives/photos/index.htm

- ***Look for enduring constants.*** Another way to introduce the concept of continuity is to identify those things that have remained constant (in some respect) for humans through the millennia. As a class, brainstorm as many elements as possible that have been present over the last 1000 years (e.g., religious beliefs, cities, roads, musical instruments).

Recognizing the positive and negative dimensions of change. The following activities may be used to help students appreciate the positive and negative dimensions of historical change.

- ***Examine positive and negative features.*** Create a T-chart on the board with the columns labeled "the best of times" and "the worst of times." Invite students to brainstorm how the present is both the best of times and the worst of times. Then, choose an era students have already studied and brainstorm similar lists for that era. The following is a partial sample of positive and negative aspects of 1920's Canada.

The 1920's

The Best of Times	The Worst of Times
• Economic boom times. • Women could vote; women's rights advanced. • The automobile increased mobility. • Radio brought the world together. • Movies expanded social awareness. • Housing was cheap.	• No formal social safety net. • Women did not have equal access to professions or pay equity. • Cities begam to expand into suburbs. • Consumerism created greedier people. • Only the wealthy could afford higher education.

Create a new chart listing the progress and decline between the 1920's and life today. Ask students to identify the most significant positive and negative changes.

- ***Examine the desirability of change from varying perspectives.*** Conclusions about the desirability of particular changes often depend on the perspective from which the changes are viewed. The prized things for some of us (e.g., rap music, MTV, less censorship in media) may be seen undesirable to others (e.g., by parents with conservative religious values, classical musicians). To reinforce the dynamic relationship between the desirability of change and a particular group's or individual's values, ask students to repeat the previously described activity as seen from various perspectives (e.g., an environmentalist, a religiously conservative parent, a poor person).

Applications across the curriculum

Once students have an understanding of continuity and change, they are then able to employ these concepts in thinking about historical events. Below are various ways in which they can be applied throughout the history curriculum.

Comparing periods. The most obvious applications of continuity and change involve students in comparing periods or conditions using either primary (e.g., newspapers, photographs) or secondary sources (e.g., textbook accounts).

- ***Focus on changes.*** An obvious approach is to ask students to notice the changes between two or more historical periods.

  For example: Direct students to contrast the courting habits of couples in 1660 in New France with those of Quebec couples in the 1950s. Students can perform a skit starting with a tableau of a wedding. Members of the wedding (e.g., the couple, their parents, friends) can tell the story of how the couple met, courted and ended up getting married.

- ***Focus on constants***. Because of a tendency to notice changes over time, it may be helpful to invite students regularly to focus their comparisons on the similarities between historical periods.

  Example: Invite students to find common elements between a typical day of a teenager in 1934 and a modern day teenager living in parallel circumstances. Students might deal with the questions in a skit, a poster, a web site construction or an essay. Questions to consider might be:

  - What were the expectations of their parents?
  - What were their living conditions? (Where did they sleep? What would they eat?)
  - What clothes did they wear? (What was fashionable?)
  - What vocational and educational expectations were typical?
  - What did the kids do for entertainment?
  - What kinds of music did they enjoy?

- ***Explore both changes and constants.*** An alternative approach is to ask students to notice the changes and similarities between historical groups or periods.

  Example. Arrange for students to research personal histories of Chinese and British immigrants in the 1870s. How were the experiences for these two immigration groups similar? How did they differ? Students might present their comparison in an annotated Venn diagram or a poster.

  Example: Using statistics from Statistics Canada and other pertinent sources, ask students to compare income levels, education, divorce, abuse, and legal rights for women in Canada for 1900 and for 2005. Based on their research, students are to compare the economic and social security of women in Canada in 1900 to the economic and social security of women today. Present the question: In what ways has progress been made in a woman's security and how has it declined or worsened? Invite students to create a PowerPoint presentation to explain and justify their views.

Tracing change and continuity over time. Another approach to integrating considerations of continuity and change is to invite students to trace historical developments over time.

- ***Identify turning points.*** Present students with a theme, such as transportation or women's rights, and invite them to trace its evolution over a period of time. Ask students to mark the main turning points in the history of the assigned phenomenon.

  Example: Present students with a timeline of ten events in the history of Canadian self-rule (e.g., elected chambers, Confederation, Statute of Westminster, repatriation of the constitution). Ask students to identify the two events that most changed Canada into a sovereign nation.

- ***Re-periodize history***. Present students with a theme (e.g., workers' rights, technology, housing) and invite them to trace its evolution over several centuries. Ask students to divide this history into periods using developments in the assigned theme as the organizing principle.

  Example: Discuss with students a traditional periodization of Canadian history organized around territorial power and political control (e.g., pre-contact, early exploration, settlement, struggle for self-rule, nation building, final independence). Suggest a different organizing concept (e.g., the role of the working class, Aboriginal well-being, the rights of women) and ask students to identify historic periods in light of this new concept.

Cause and consequence

5

On April 19, 1884, the Indian Act was amended to make it a criminal offence to participate in a Potlatch:

> *Every Indian or other person who engages in or assists in celebrating the Indian festival known as the 'Potlatch'...is guilty of a misdemeanour, and liable to imprisonment for a term of not more than six months and no less than two months.*

Why would the government prohibit this custom and what were the consequences of this action? The First Nations who practiced the Potlatch did no harm others in their ceremonies and in fact it served as a social safety net being a major means for redistributing wealth. According to the Indian Commissioner, the lavish giving and feasting undermined civic values:

> *They [Native people of the West Coast of Vancouver Island] are a hardy and industrious race, and so far as I could perceive the richest of any Indians I have met in the Province. Were a proper disposal made of their immense gains they could, without a doubt, live independently, and furnish themselves with every comfort, and every luxury to be wished for ... On such occasions [potlatches] a large amount of property is given away or destroyed, and the continual round of feasting ... is quite destructive to any settled habit of labor and industry ... They care very little for agriculture.*[1]

To the First Nations this explanation seemed contradictory:

> *We see in this a contradictory state of affairs adorning your civilization. Churches are numerous; theatres are located in the various sections of the town; saloons multiply in numbers; all of which are in conformity with your laws ... You have your Christmas, First of July and 24th of May, all of which your celebrate without interference ... Money is spent in squandrous profusion with no benefit to the poor of your race ... We see in your graveyards the white marble and granite monuments which cost you money in testimony of your grief for the dead.*[2]

The questions raised by this incident include: What were the real reasons for prohibiting the Potlatch? What effect did this ban have on First Nations communities? Did the prohibition achieve its intended result? The answers to these questions draw attention to cause and consequence in history.

The concepts of cause and consequence address who or what influenced history and what were the repercussions of these changes. By "who" we mean individuals, groups and social movements. The "what" refers to ideologies, institutions and other systemic

---

[1] I.W. Powell, *Annual Report,* Department of Indian Affairs, Ottawa, 1875.

[2] Petition of Rights drawn up by a delegation of Native people in *The Daily Columbian,* New Westminster, February 26, 1896.

factors. Some events are caused by intentional acts carried out by individual and groups to bring about change (e,g., the passing of legislation to ban the Potlatch). Other causes are the result of accident, omission or broader societal factors that are unintended (e.g., the stock market crash in 1929). The challenge for students is to understand the role human agency and social, economic, political, and environmental forces play in shaping the course of history and then to trace the consequences of these events.

Dimensions of cause and consequence

Key aspects for students' understanding of cause and consequence are usefully summarized by the following principles:

Events have a myriad of different and often unappreciated causes. Although some causes are more significant than others, it is important for students to appreciate that events rarely have a single or even just a few causes. In reducing the study of historical influences to the few most significant, students often lose sight of the dynamic interplay of factors. In the case of the prohibition of the Potlatch, for example, the causes stated above were economic and social in nature. But evidence of religious and cultural influences are suggested in the following passage:

> *The feasts were followed by wild rites, and devil-dances, at which the demon-scaring masks, huge helmets of cedar sculpture with grotesque carvings were worn. Still, it is said, the great brown cedars of the northern coast witness, sometimes, these pagan picnics ... The dark influence of the medicine men is still stronger than that of the missionaries. The ancient fetishism is still stronger than the gentle religion taught by the missionaries.*[3]

Also important is student appreciation of the unrecognized influences of groups that typically are excluded from historical narratives and school texts. For example, minority groups, women and working people are rarely given as much credit for historical change as are political, industrial and military leaders (e.g., Who really built the CPR?).

Prior events may have no causal influence on subsequent events. Simply because an event preceded another does not mean that the prior event caused or contributed to the subsequent event. For example, if I left the house angry after having a dispute with my spouse and subsequently get in a car accident, we should presume that the marital rift contributed to the accident. It may have influenced the outcome; but then again, the accident may have had nothing to do with my being distracted. In attributing causal relationships, it is not sufficient that one event precedes another; students must look for evidence that would link the two events. For example, the expansion of the Canadian Pacific Railway and the joining of British Columbia in Confederation preceded the ban on the Potlatch. Yet these earlier events may not have had any causal influence on the ban. In establishing a causal link students would need to find evidence connecting these events to an increased political and social will to assimilate First Nations people.

---

[3] Polloug Pogue, "Potlatches" *The Vancouver Sun,* August 29, 1913.

Looking for broad underlying factors is as or more important than identifying immediate particular causes. Any event will have particular immediate causes—for example, a car accident may be caused by slippery roads and a failure to use a turn signal to indicate an intended change of lanes. Behind these specific factors are found more fundamental influences—perhaps, a general recklessness on the part of drivers, a failure to maintain roads so they do not become greasy, a culture of speed that precipitates these kinds of incidents. These broader influences are often referred to as underlying causes. These are explanatory concepts that relate to societal forces more generally. For example, historians' efforts to uncover why the Potlatch was banned will go beyond the personal explanations of the Indian Commissioner and other individuals even though their expressed motives quite likely influenced their actions. Historians would want to examine the underlying factors behind mainstream resistance to the Potlatch. Perhaps, these motives stem from a desire by the majority European culture to assimilate aboriginal culture. This might be traced to economic and social concerns associated with the impediments that Aboriginal title presented to western development. If First Nations peoples were assimilated then their demands for separate territory, self-government and economic rights would disappear.

Actions have unintended consequences. Studying about unanticipated consequences is as important as examining whether or not the intended results were achieved. A famous example of unintended consequence is the impact of the elevator on urban density. Towering commercial and residential buildings which characterize the landscape of most large cities would not have been possible were it not for the elevator. Likewise, the invention of the Internet, which started as a closed communication network among university and government institutions, has begun to transform the economic and social structure of our planet. So too, the banning of the Potlatch which might have been intended to assimilate First Nations peoples into the majority European culture and economy had unforeseen consequences. Rather than assimilating into the mainstream society, many First Nations people were further estranged from it.

Introducing the concepts to students

Before examining cause and consequence in various aspects of their study of history, it will be useful to introduce students to these concepts.

Distinguishing causes from antecedent events and consequences from after-the-fact events. Students must learn to distinguish the causes of an event from antecedent events and the subsequent consequences from unrelated incidents that followed an event. One strategy is to provide a list of events associated with a familiar incident (e.g., below is a list of pre- and post-events associated with the Prince's marriage to Cinderella in the familiar fairytale). Ask students to sort these events into four categories: causes, antecedent events, consequences, and subsequent events.

- Cinderella is mistreated by her step-mother and step-sisters.
- Cinderella is not allowed to go to the ball.
- The fairy godmother magically makes Cinderella a gown and carriage so she can go to the ball, but she warns Cinderella that they will revert back to common materials at midnight.

- Cinderella meets the Prince at the ball.
- The Prince and Cinderella dance.
- The Prince is smitten by Cinderella's beauty and charm.
- Cinderella runs away from the ball at midnight before the magical spell that has created her dress and carriage runs out, but she loses her glass slipper in her hasty exit.
- The Prince discovers that Cinderella's foot is the only one in his kingdom that will fit the glass slipper.
- The Prince and Cinderella live happily every after.
- Cinderella is freed from the oppression of her step-mother and step-sisters.
- The old King dies and the Prince is crowned King.

Distinguishing immediate causes from underlying factors. Present students with an everyday scenario such as the one outlined below. Invite students to discuss the causes of the incident. Encourage students to distinguish between particular personal causes (e.g., the victim had run out of cigarettes, the victim was hit by a car) and broader social influences (e.g., lax law enforcement, indifference to public safety).

> Just before midnight one dark and stormy night, a man called John Smith, an engine mechanic, was sitting in an isolated cabin in the woods. As he reached for a cigarette, he noticed he had only one left. Glancing at his watch, he realized that he had just enough time to hop in his car, and drive to the gas station down the road to buy cigarettes before it closed. As his car pulled out of his lane and onto the highway, it was hit by his neighbour, who, returning from a long night of drinking, was unable to stop his car soon enough on the icy road. Smith was killed instantly. Later, as the townspeople were discussing the sad event, they shook their heads one after another and said, "We always knew that smoking would kill Smith." It is worth noting that local officials had long been warned of the dangers of that part of the highway, especially in winter, and yet they seemed uninterested in doing anything about it. Apparently because the residents of that part of the town did not have any influence with local authorities. Others wondered if the liquor laws had been more faithfully enforced in the town whether the neighbour who smashed into Smith would have been as drunk as was.[4]

Recognizing different types of causes. To help students appreciate the diverse range of influences affecting any given event, present the class with a familiar scenario such as the one described above. Invite students to identify the types of causes (e.g., economic, political, psychological environmental, cultural) contributing to the incident.

---

[8] Taken from *Heaven & Hell on Earth: The Massacre of the "Black" Donnellys,* part of the Great Unsolved Mysteries in Canadian History series: www.canadianmysteries.ca

Applications across the curriculum

Once students have an understanding of cause and consequence, they can then employ these concepts when thinking about historical events. Below are various ways in which they can be applied throughout the history curriculum.

Exploring human agency. An important aspect of historical causation is the role of human effort in bring about and resisting change.

- ***Identify critical agents***. Invite students to identify a contemporary social issue or conflict (e.g., First Nations land claims, gay marriage, the role of the Senate in Canada, conflict in the Middle East, the environment, AIDS, universal health care, class size). Next ask students to identify who could play a lead role in determining the eventual resolution of the assigned issues. Encourage students to identify individuals and organizations that might bring about change as well as individuals, institutions and other forces that might restrain these changes. After constructing a comprehensive list, ask students to decide which agents are most critical to the outcome of these struggles. Discuss the factors that enhance or reduce an agent's influence in a particular struggle.

  Example: Arrange for students to prepare a magazine article on the forces behind the building of the Canadian Pacific Railway. Include the role of following historical agents in their account:

  - political leaders (e.g., John A. Macdonald)
  - financial leaders (e.g., Donald Smith, George Stephen)
  - managers (e.g., William Van Horne)
  - builders (e.g., Major A.B. Rogers, James Ross)
  - negotiators (e.g., Crowfoot)
  - workers (e.g., Irish navies, Chinese workers)

  In the article, students should indicate which agents were the most crucial to the eventual completion of the CPR.

- ***Compare intentions with results***. Encourage students to examine the relationship between an individual agent's objectives and the eventual consequences of the actions. There are many instances in history where "the best laid plans have gone awry".

  Example: Invite students to create a docudrama about Prime Minister Mulroney and his attempt to remove the threat of Quebec separation from Canada through the Meech Lake and Charlottetown Accords. Encourage students to construct interviews of Mulroney, based on his actual speeches and interviews, about what he hoped to accomplish by the Meech Lake and Charlottetown Accords. Students might also construct an interview with Lucien Bouchard about the consequences of Meech Lake and Charlottetown on the desire for separation in Quebec.

Identifying significant causes. There are many opportunities in the curriculum for students to explore the historical causes of events.

- ***Distinguish cause and consequences.*** Provide students with a list of possible causes and invite them to identify those factors that are causes they can directly link to the event as a cause.

  Example: Ask students to decide which of the following factors were causes of the "Great Depression" in Canada and which were antecedent events, consequences or subsequent (unconnected) events.

  - the Stock Market Crash of 1929;
  - the "Dust Bowl" in the prairies in the 1930's;
  - overproduction as the industrial capacity of the U.S.A. and Canada expanded beyond the ability of the consumer to consume;
  - economic nationalism and tariffs;
  - international debt;
  - unemployment;
  - World War II.

  Students must explain the connection between the attributed causes and the Great Depression. Several of these factors can be tied directly as causes of the "Great Depression". Overproduction was a readily identifiable central cause as it created a surplus of products resulting in lower prices, lost profit, factory closures and unemployment. Others such as the "Dust bowl" were ecological disasters that contributed to the poverty of the Depression but were not a direct cause. In fact agricultural over-production was a greater cause of the Depression. The Stock Market Crash could be argued to be an indicator of problems to come but was not a direct cause of the Depression. Unemployment was a consequence of the Depression rather than a cause of it.

- ***Rank order key causes.*** Instead of asking students simply to list the main causes of an event, direct them to rank the events in order of important or effect on the outcome.

  Example: Present students with the following list of five causes of World War II.[5] In groups, ask students to rank order these events and explain their reasons for the ranking.

  - the Depression,
  - rise of totalitarian dictatorships,
  - appeasement,
  - isolationism,
  - the Treaty of Versailles.

- ***Explore causal interconnections.*** To help students appreciate the dynamic interactions among causal factors, invite them to create a web diagramming the interaction of events. Students could place the causes on a piece of paper, on the board or on an overhead and draw circles around them. Vary the size of the circle to represent the magnitude of the significance of the event. Students can then draw arrows connecting various circles and annotate those arrows with a short description of how one event affected the other.

[5] Based on an activity developed by Oliver Sandor, a student teacher at the University of British Columbia, in the Spring of 2006.

Example: Present students with the list of causes of World War II suggested in the previous example. Ask students to illustrate the interconnection of these causes using a web. Such a diagram might look like the one below. Ask students to explain their analysis of the interacting causes.

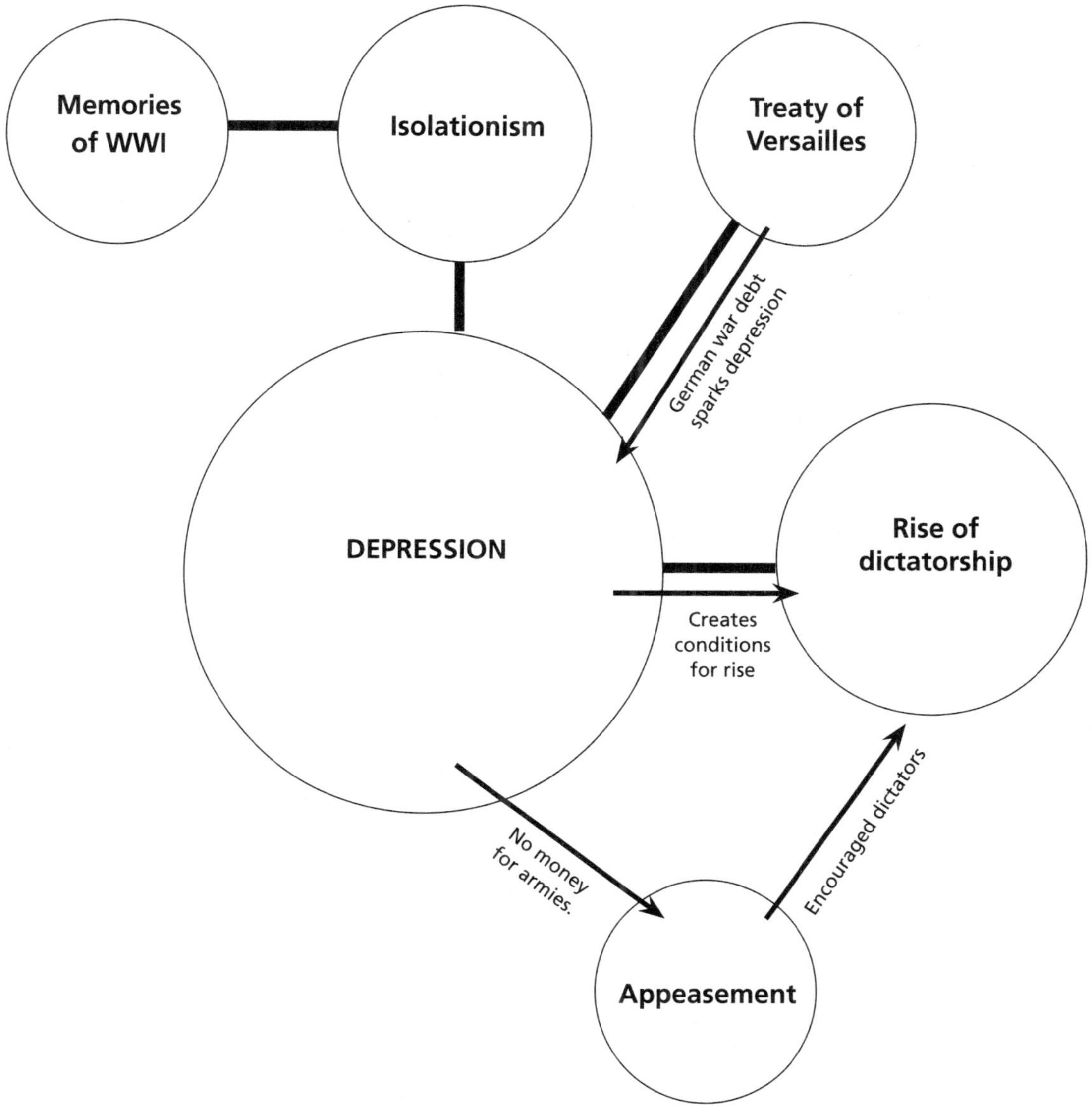

- ***Examine constraints on actions***. In addition to examining why events happened, it is also instructive to invite students to consider why certain events didn't happen (e.g., What prevented Hitler from winning the war? Why did the US not take over Canada?).

  Example: Invite students to explore the constraints (especially economic and political) that prevented Newfoundland from remaining a colony of Britain in 1949. Alternatively, consider why Newfoundland didn't join the U.S. despite the considerable influence it had in the colony.

Examining consequences. It is important that students consider not only the causes of historical events but also their consequences.

- ***Identify direct and indirect consequences***. Introduce students to the concepts of *direct* and *indirect* consequences. Direct consequences are the immediate results of a situation (e.g., bleeding is a direct result of cutting a finger, feeling cold is a direct result of going outside in the winter). Indirect consequences emerge as a result of some other consequence. For example, staining one's shirt with blood is an indirect consequence of cutting a finger; getting sick is an indirect consequences of going outside in the winter. These are indirect consequences: if cutting a finger didn't have the direct consequence of lots of blood, then the shirt would not have become stained; similarly, if going outside in the winter hadn't resulted in the person feeling cold, then the person would not have become sick. Ask students to brainstorm consequences of an assigned historical event and then distinguish the direct from the indirect consequences. Encourage students to see that indirect consequences can themselves give rise to yet further consequences. The important point is not to correctly label every consequence but to appreciate how a particular event can have ripple effects throughout society and over time. To help students visualize these ripple effects, you may suggest they web the direct and indirect consequences of an assigned event using the diagram *Web of effects* (Blackline Master #8) found at the back of this volume.

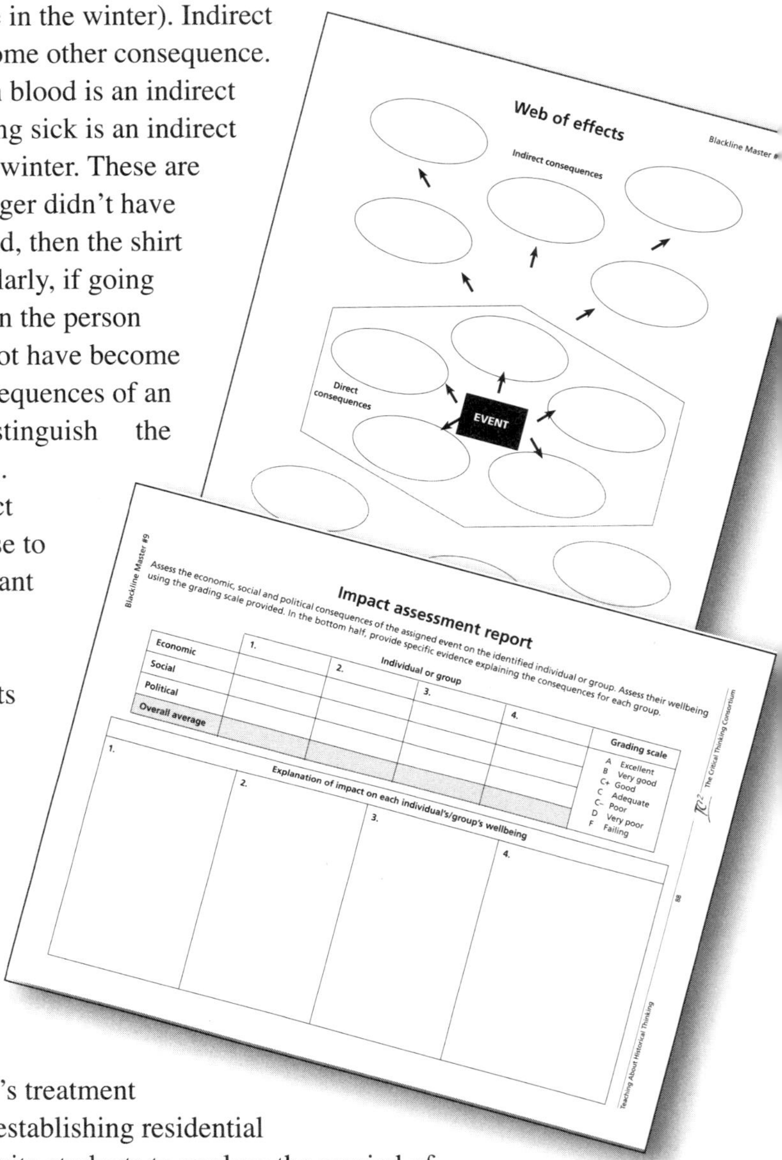

  Example: Select a landmark event in the history of the federal government's treatment of Canada's Aboriginal people (e.g., establishing residential schools, banning the Potlatch) and invite students to explore the myriad of personal, social, economic, cultural, and legal consequences (direct and indirect) of this event.

- ***Assess the impact.*** Instead of simply asking students to identify consequences, invite them to draw overall conclusions about the impact of events on one or more groups or individuals. One method of assessing historical impact is to construct a values time-line. Rather than a straight line, a values time-line tracks events according to their impact on the target group on a range from very positive to very negative. Alternatively, students might create a report card where they assign grades (from A+ to F) to rate the impact of an event on the economic, political and social wellbeing of one or more target groups. You may want to suggest a format such as the one found in *Impact assessment report* (Blackline Master #9) at the back of this resource.

Example: Identify with students a number of landmark events in the history of the federal government's treatment of Canada's Aboriginal people (e.g., establishing residential schools, prohibition of the Potlatch, closing of residential schools). Direct students to research the implications of each event on Aboriginal peoples and then to plot the events along the line and rate each on a scale (+2 to –2) according to its impact.

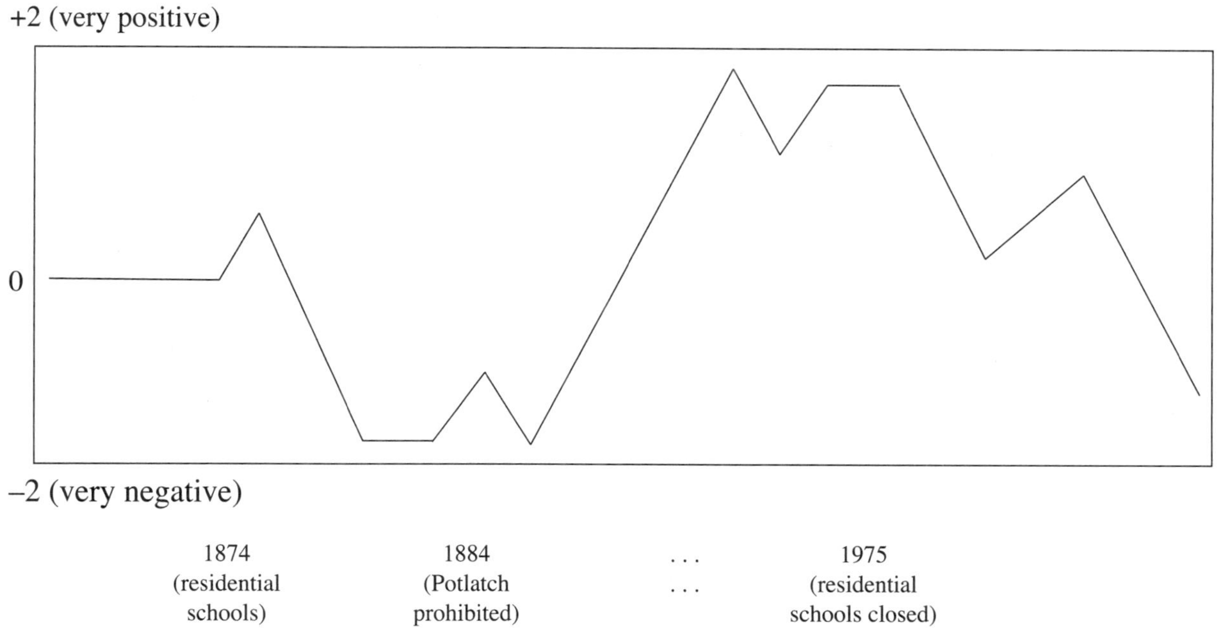

- ***Examine what might have happened if things had worked out differently.*** The use of counterfactual or alternative histories are effective in helping students appreciate the myriad consequences of an event. In constructing a counterfactual history, students must explain what would most likely have happened had a certain event not occurred (e.g., if the colonies did not join Confederation in 1867) or had turned out differently (e.g., if the French had won the Battle of the Plains of Abraham instead of the British).

  Example: Invite students to consider what might have occurred had the 1995 referendum on Quebec's independence gone the other way. Explain to the class that sovereignty was defeated by a small margin (50.58% voting "No" and 49.42% voting "Yes"). A record 94% of registered Quebecers voted in the referendum. Sovereignty was the choice of Francophones by a majority of about 60%. It would have taken very little for the referendum to pass. In fact, if the vote had been taken a week earlier, it might well have done so. Encourage students to research what various agents (e.g., Jean Chrétien, Jacques Parizeau, other provincial premiers) were contemplating in the event that the referendum passed. Direct students to identify several counterfactual scenarios and find evidence to support the likelihood of each. Such scenarios might include the following:

  - The federal government of Canada might have peacefully negotiated a separation with Quebec along the lines of the division of Czechoslovakia into the Czech and Slovak republics.
  - The federal government might have refused to accept the results because the question was not clear-cut, and ordered a national referendum on Quebec sovereignty.

- Other provinces might have held their own referendums and opted for sovereignty with perhaps British Columbia and Alberta forming a separate republic.
- The federal government might have refused to recognize Quebec sovereignty and sent in the troops.

Ask students to select and justify their choice for the most likely scenario and to explore the plausible implications for Canada and Quebec of this scenario.

Historical perspective

6

Susanna Moodie (1803-1884) in her famous memoir, *Roughing it in the Bush,* describes the following reactions to the people her family encountered in their newly adopted country:

All was new, strange, and distasteful to us; we shrank from the rude, coarse familiarity of the uneducated people among whom we were thrown; and they in return viewed us as innovators, who wished to curtail their independence, by expecting from them the kindly civilities and gentle courtesies of a more refined community. They considered us proud and shy when we were only anxious not to give offence. The semi-barbarous Yankee squatters, who had "left their country for their country's good," and by whom we were surrounded in our first settlement, detested us, and with them we could have no feeling in common. We could neither lie nor cheat in our dealings with them; and they despised us for our ignorance in trading and our want of smartness. . . .

But from this folly the native-born Canadian is exempt; it is only practised by the low-born Yankee, or the Yankeefied British peasantry and mechanics. It originates in the enormous reaction springing out of a sudden emancipation from a state of utter dependence to one of unrestrained liberty. As such, I not only excuse, but forgive it, for the principle is founded in nature; and, however disgusting and distasteful to those accustomed to different treatment from their inferiors, it is better than a hollow profession of duty and attachment urged upon us by a false and unnatural position. Still, it is very irksome until you think more deeply upon it; and then it serves to amuse rather than to irritate.

And here I would observe, before quitting this subject, that of all follies, that of taking out servants from the old country is one of the greatest, and is sure to end in the loss of the money expended in their passage, and to become the cause of deep disappointment and mortification to yourself.

They no sooner set foot upon the Canadian shores than they become possessed with this ultra-republican spirit. All respect for their employers, all subordination, is at all end; the very air of Canada severs the tie of mutual obligation which bound you together. They fancy themselves not only equal to you in rank, but that ignorance and vulgarity give them superior claims to notice. They demand in terms the highest wages, and grumble at doing half the work, in return, which they cheerfully performed at home. They demand to eat at your table, and to sit in your company; and if you refuse to listen to their dishonest and extravagant claims, they tell you that "they are free; that no contract signed in the old country is binding in 'Meriky;' that you may look out for another person to fill their place as soon as you like; and that you may get the money expended in their passage and outfit in the best manner you can.[1]

[1] S. Moodie, 1852. *Roughing it in the Bush.* London: Richard Bentley (Volume I, Chapter XI).

Susanna Moodie's reactions to the people in her new home country raise questions on two levels—what exactly is she saying and what conclusions should we draw from these descriptions. More specifically, what does it mean to say her family was looked upon as "innovators" and that they curtailed the "independence" of others simply because they expected their neighbours to exhibit "kindly civilities and gentle courtesies." Clearly, Moodie regards herself as better educated than her fellow Canadians, yet she claims without regret to lack "smartness." And what is implied by the "ultra-republican spirit" exhibited by those "servants from the old country" when they became immigrants?

Even after we fathom the intended meaning of these expressions, we are left to draw conclusions about the people and events described. Does Moodie's surprise that the immigrant servants fancied themselves her equal and her disdain that they should expect to talk and eat with their employers, suggest she was an elitist snob mired in Old World norms? She seems to understand why "all respect for their employers, all subordination, is at all end" and she can not only "excuse" but she can "forgive it". On the other hand, she readily identifies with her class structure when she refers to "the low-born Yankee, or the Yankeefied British peasantry and mechanics." We are left asking, within the values of her world, whether she was socially progressive or patronizing. More generally, we might wonder what it was like to live in this confluence of Old and New World values and manners.

Any attempt to answer these questions raises issues of historical perspective. The past is a "foreign country" and thus is it difficult to understand what was meant by and what we can legitimately conclude from the clues that remain from these bygone times. Our attempts at historical understanding are often clouded by our current concerns, beliefs and values because our natural tendency when looking at past events is to apply a contemporary perspective.

Historical perspective involves the viewing of the past through the social, intellectual, emotional and moral lenses of the time. Historical perspective requires that we remain mindful of the potentially profound differences between our own worldview and that of past worldviews.

Dimensions of historical perspective

The central elements of students' understanding of historical perspective are usefully summarized by the following principles:

Presentism is the antithesis of historical perspective. Presentism is the imposition of a contemporary perspective when interpreting events in the past. Asking students to imagine how they would feel if they were a particular historical person is more likely to undermine historical perspective taking than it is to advance it. Students often presume that people were always like us or, perhaps, they simply don't know better. As such, students are inclined to apply modern lenses that distort the past and what it meant for the people living at the time. This problem is exacerbated by popular historical films that recreate past times dressed in the manners, values and customs of our times. Coming to grips with the idea that "reality" was different for other people in other times is both one of the most fascinating and challenging tasks in history. At the most basic level, this means students should not presume that the words used in historical documents mean the same to the people who wrote them as they do to us who read them now. And it certainly requires that students, when drawing conclusions about the past, become informed about and remain conscious of the values, beliefs and customs of the time. Rather than asking students to project how they would feel if they were an historical person, we want to ask students to imagine how the person must think and feel as a product of her time.

Historical perspective is concerned with understanding the prevailing norms of the time more than it is adopting a particular person's point of view. Though it is sometimes called "historical empathy," historical perspective is very different from the common-sense notion of emotionally feeling for or identifying with another person. In fact, historical perspective taking is less a matter of getting inside an individual person's head or heart (unless, of course, one is writing a personal biography) than it is getting inside the collective mindset of the times. Susanna Moodie did not invent her point of view, but acquired it as part of the worldview of her British social class and her new, more egalitarian society. It is that worldview, rather than Moodie's personal perspective, that we truly want to understand.

There are diverse historical perspectives on any given event in the past. As the adage goes "there are two sides to every coin," and the same can be said of historical perspectives. There is no universal perspective operating at any given time in history. Moodie's attitudes towards American and British servant class immigrants may have been widely shared by people in her social circles, but many others would have rejected her viewpoint. And, it is certainly true that the Americans' perspectives and the British servant's perspectives on their behaviour would differ greatly from Moodie's characterization.

Adopting an historical perspective requires suspending moral judgment. When we pass judgment on a person or event, to some extent we stand outside that event or person. However, the point of assuming an historical perspective is to enter into that person's or event's frame of reference. To this extent, historical perspective taking requires suspending moral judgment. This does not imply that students endorse the meanings, values and ideas of the past, but rather that they understand why people and societies from other times might have held them and how these views informed their perspective on the events and people of the time. For example, Susanna Moodie's class consciousness is not something we are sympathetic to today. However, we must try to understand a world where "inferiors"—those with less education and wealth—were expected to show deference to their "betters" perhaps in the way that children today are expected to show deference to their seniors. The point of assuming an historical perspective is not to dismiss Moodie's expectations as acts of snobbery but to understand what these values were and what it meant to those who held them to have those values challenged by others.

Introducing the concept to students

Before examining historical perspectives in various aspects of their study of history, it will be useful to assist students in learning to assume the perspective of others and to recognize the challenges of doing this.

Assuming the perspectives of others. One way to introduce the idea of differing perspectives is to ask students to assume perspectives on events familiar to them. Structure this activity by creating a three-column chart. Label the first column "topic", the second "my parents' view" and the third "my view". In the first column, invite students to list topics on which their perceptions and their parents' differ (e.g., music, friends, freedom of movement, curfews, fashion). In the other two columns, ask students to detail the differences between their viewpoints and those of their parents. Explore a number of topics and discuss why these differences may exist (e.g., life experience, priorities). If desired, repeat this activity by inviting students to assume the perspectives of various interest groups on a topical social issue (e.g., school uniforms, young drivers, safe sex).

Anticipating different meanings. One of the challenges in reading historical texts is the fact that the common meaning of words today are often different from the meanings those words had in the past. One way to sensitize students to this fact is to scrutinize an historical text such as the above-cited passage from *Roughing it in the Bush.* Ask students to read each sentence looking for clues that suggest which words may not have the same meaning to Susanna Moodie that they have for us today. Encourage students to read the context of the surrounding sentences to try to infer a more likely historical meaning. For example, Moodie's reference to her lack of "smartness" comes in the context of her inability to lie and cheat and her naiveté about the ways of business. After speculating about possible historical meanings, direct students to a dictionary, such as the *Oxford English Dictionary,* that describes the etymology of words. As it turns out, a meaning of 'smartness', first reported about the time Moodie was writing her journal, suggests excessive shrewdness, especially for one's own advantage (*OED*, 1986, 2878). The implied differences between the two philosophies of commerce (e.g., fair dealings versus get away with as much as one can) are instructive. The point of the activity is not to require students to look up every "curious" word, but to teach students to identify which words may not be used according to contemporary understandings.

Exploring the "foreignness" of perspectives. When assuming an historical perspective students must be willing to attempt to make sense of historical practices and beliefs that may seem strange or incomprehensible. One strategy for nurturing this attitude is to present students with cultural practices that may be unfamiliar and perhaps seem odd. For example, mention you have heard of a cultural group that made baby diapers out of moss, plays soccer at three in the morning, and used fish to make runners for a sled. After soliciting students' initial reactions, explain the context and rationale for the practices. These Inuit practices make sense within a harsh northern environment. Moss was used traditionally as a form of diaper because it was free, biodegradable, widely available and had hygienic properties. After being restricted during the long winter, playing soccer at night makes sense in the few summer months when there is endless daylight. Frozen fish was a cheap and replaceable source of material when building a traditional sled to travel on ice and snow. Draw attention to the fact that these initially "foreign" practices make sense when we understand their context and rationale. Discuss the difficulties presented in historical contexts when we may not have access to this background information and that we can often only speculate what the practices and beliefs actually meant to the people who held them.

Applications across the curriculum

Once students appreciate the importance of and obstacles to assuming an historical perspective, they can then employ this concept when thinking about historical events throughout the history curriculum.

Explain an historical person's perspective. One way to begin to involve students in historical perspective taking is to provide several documents by someone from another time and ask students to try to explain the author's perspective.

Example: Provide students with selected excerpts from *Roughing It In The Bush* by Susanna Moodie. Invite students to focus their attention on understanding Moodie's social environment. What limitations did Moodie face? How might they have affected her perspective? What seemed to be most important to her? How did she handle various situations? Why did she handle them that way? How would her worldview and values differ from those of students today?

Anticipate an historical person's perspective. One of the most popular approaches to historical perspective taking is to ask students to anticipate an assigned person's views or thoughts on a particular topic. Typically, students are asked to write a letter or diary entry, or create a drawing or poster from that perspective. For reasons stated above, it is important to clarify whether the purpose is to develop compassion for the plight of an individual or to develop historical perspective. If the latter objective is intended, then encourage students to focus on the broader social norms and beliefs that underlie the person's perspective and less on the particular emotions the individual might feel. You may want to use a structure such as the one suggested on *Historical profile* (Blackline Master #10) where students locate their assigned person's attitudes on a range of broad social issues prior to developing a perspective on a particular matter. It would be important for students to acquire the historical context for the perspective they are expected to adopt by accessing sources provided by the teacher or that they would locate.

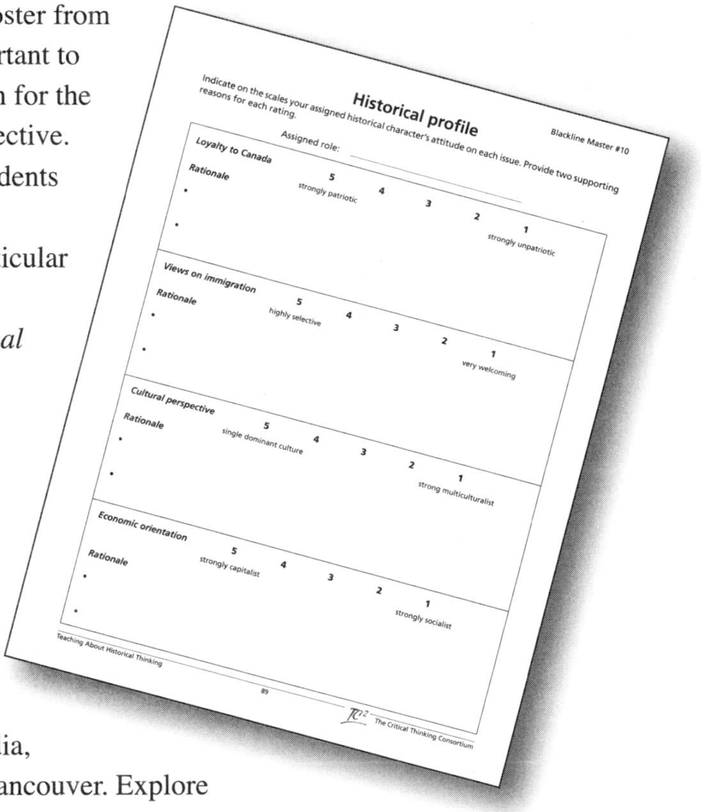
Historical profile
Blackline Master #10
Indicate on the scales your assigned historical character's attitude on each issue. Provide two supporting reasons for each rating.
Assigned role:

Loyalty to Canada	5 strongly patriotic	4	3	2	1 strongly unpatriotic	Rationale
Views on immigration	5 highly selective	4	3	2	1 very welcoming	Rationale
Cultural perspective	5 single dominant culture	4	3	2	1 strong multiculturalist	Rationale
Economic orientation	5 strongly capitalist	4	3	2	1 strongly socialist	Rationale

Teaching About Historical Thinking
89
The Critical Thinking Consortium

Example: In 1914, the *Komagata Maru*, a steamship carrying hopeful immigrants from India, was not allowed to discharge its passengers in Vancouver. Explore the prevailing attitudes surrounding this issue by asking students to assume one of 33 historical roles drawn from a cross-section of Canadian society (e.g., Boer War veteran, Japanese fisherman, health nurse, Aboriginal woman). As preparation, brief students on the general conditions in the early 1900s and the specific events leading to the arrival of the *Komagata Maru*. To help students assume the perspectives of their assigned individual, ask them to speculate on their character's attitudes on issues such as loyalty to Canada, immigration, cultural assimilation and economics. See below for a sample answer and accompanying rationale suggesting the attitudes a veteran of the Boer War might hold on these issues. (A blank version of this chart, which students would complete for their assigned historical character is found in Blackline Master #10.) Next, ask students to develop arguments for and against accepting the *Komagata Maru* passengers from the perspective of their assigned character. In role, students debate whether or not the passengers should have been accepted into Canada and then write a letter justifying their historical character's position.[2]

Boer War veteran profile

Role: British Boer War veteran | **Personal data:** *war colonel; strong British imperialist*

	5	4	3	2	1
Loyalty to Canada	5	4	(3)	2	1
	strongly patriotic				strongly unpatriotic

Rationale
- he is likely a strong monarchist and British nationalist because he fought for Britain in the Boer War;
- his ties to Canada may lie more with its membership in the British Empire than with any deep patriotism.

Views on immigration	5	(4)	3	2	1
	highly selective				very welcoming

Rationale
- if he is British and upper class, he would likely favour immigrants from the British Empire, including those from India;
- fighting in South Africa during the Boer War may have created a low estimation of the worthiness of non-British people.

Cultural perspective	5	(4)	3	2	1
	single dominant culture				strong multiculturalist

Rationale
- being a strong British imperialist suggests he would strongly favour immigrants abandoning their cultural traditions for the behaviour and values of English-Canadian society;
- possibly influenced by Rudyard Kipling he may hold the view that "British is better".

Economic orientation	5	(4)	3	2	1
	strongly capitalist				strongly unionist

Rationale
- as a colonel he may not have had much experience as a labourer or appreciate the value of unions;
- because he is not an independent business owner he may not have strong capitalist ties, but may appreciate the economic benefits that industry and business provide.

[2] Detailed instructions and resources for this activity are found in C. Misfeldt and R. Case. 2003. *Immigration in 20th century Canada*. Vancouver: The Critical Thinking Consortium, pp 17-24.

Explore differing historical perspectives. Encourage examination of the diversity of historical perspectives by inviting students to assume different sides on a conflict. Provide students with primary or secondary sources representing differing perspectives on a given event. Invite students to identify and explain their differences.

Example. Students might explore the divergent views on slavery within Canada and the US by creating dramatic monologues where the perspectives of slaves, slave owners and abolitionists are represented. You might suggest a special role for George Brown, the founder of the Anti-Slavery Society of Canada. In preparation, direct students to research the following questions:

- What rules governed American slave owners and slaves? (Look at the Missouri Compromise, the Dred Scott Case, and the *Fugitive Slave Act*.)
- How was slavery justified in a democracy? (Read the beginning of the Declaration of Independence. How could the founding fathers of the U.S. declare a war for their own independence while enslaving a large part of their own population? How was it slavery, a widespread practice at the time, wasn't even mentioned in the U.S. Constitution?)
- How did people work toward its abolition? (Harriet Tubman and the Underground Railroad and the Anti-Slavery Society of Canadaand Abolitionist groups in the US.)
- How did Canada become a haven for slaves? (Look at the British *Emancipation Act*.)

Moral judgment

7

In October 1970, the Front de Libération du Québec kidnapped British Trade Commissioner James Cross and Quebec Justice Minister Pierre Laporté. On October 12th, armed forces were sent to guard Ottawa. The following interview with then Prime Minister Pierre Elliot Trudeau took place the day after the troop deployment. [1]

Q: *Sir, what is it with all these men with guns around here?*

A: *Haven't you noticed?*

Q: *Yes, I've noticed them. I wondered why you people decided to have them.*

A: *What's your worry?...*

Q: *I'm worried about living in a town that's full of people with guns running around.*

A: *Why? Have they done anything to you? Have they pushed you around or anything?*

Q: *They've pushed around friends of mine. ... Doesn't it worry you, having a town that you've got to resort to this kind of thing?*

A: *It doesn't worry me. I think it's natural that if people are being abducted that they be protected against such abductions. What would you do if a Quebec minister - another Quebec minister were abducted or a federal minister? ...*

Q: *But with your army troops you seem to be combating them almost as though it is a war, and if it is a war does anything that they say have validity?*

A: *Don't be silly. We're not combating them as if it's war but we're using some of the army as peace agents in order that the police be more free to do their job as policemen and not spend their time guarding your friends against some form of kidnapping.*

Q: *You said earlier that you would protect them in this way but you have said before that this kind of violence, what you're fighting here, the kind of violence of the FLQ, can lead to a police state.*

A: *Sure. That's what you're complaining about, isn't it?...*

Q: *And one of the things I have to give up for that choice is the fact that people like you may be kidnapped.*

A: *Sure, but this isn't my choice, obviously. You know, I think it is more important to get rid of those who are committing violence against the total society and those who are trying to run the government through a parallel power by establishing their authority by kidnapping and blackmail. And I think it is our duty as a government to protect government officials and important people in our society against being used as tools in*

[1] Impromptu interview of Pierre Elliott Trudeau with Tim Ralfe of the CBC and Peter Reilly of CJON-TV on October 13, 1970. Transcribed from "'Just watch me'". *The CBC Digital Archives Website*. Canadian Broadcasting Corporation. Last updated: 13 Oct. 2005. <http://archives.cbc.ca/IDC-1-71-162-429/conflict_war/twt/clip1>.

this blackmail. Now, you don't agree to this but I am sure that once again with hindsight, you would probably have found it preferable if Mr Cross and Mr Laporte had been protected from kidnapping, which they weren't because these steps we re taking now weren't taken. But even with your hindsight I don't see how you can deny that.

Q: *No, I still go back to the choice that you have to make in the kind of society that you live in.*

A: *Yes, well there are a lot of bleeding hearts around who just don't like to see people with helmets and guns. All I can say is, go on and bleed, but it is more important to keep law and order in the society than to be worried about weak-kneed people who don't like the looks of ...*

Q: *At any cost? How far would you go with that? How far would you extend that?*

A: *Well just watch me.*

Q: *At reducing civil liberties? To what extent?*

A: *To what extent?*

Q: *Well, if you extend this and you say, ok, you're going to do anything to protect them, does this include wire-tapping, reducing other civil liberties in some way?*

A: *Yes, I think the society must take every means at its disposal to defend itself against the emergence of a parallel power which defies the elected power in this country and I think that goes to any distance. So long as there is a power in here which is challenging the elected representative of the people I think that power must be stopped and I think it's only, I repeat, weak-kneed bleeding hearts who are afraid to take these measures.*

On October 15th, troops were sent into Quebec to help the police, and on October 16th, the federal government invoked the *War Measures Act*, suspending civil liberties. While most politicians and citizens accepted the need to deploy troops, many felt invoking the *War Measures Act* during peace time was an unwarranted over-reaction and posed a dangerous precedent.

The lingering issue from this infamous incident in Canadian history is whether or not Prime Minister Trudeau was justified in declaring the *War Measures Ac*t. This is a question of moral judgment. In history, *moral judgments are attempts to make ethical assessments of the past or of implications of past actions in light of our present values and sensibilities and with consideration of the norms and conditions operating at the time of the events.*

Dimensions of moral judgment

The various aspects that are central to students' understanding of moral judgment are usefully summarized by the following principles:

Moral judgments are a particular kind of evaluative (or value) judgment. Not all historical judgments are moral judgments. Judgments can be of many kinds:

- economic (e.g., free trade was a great boon to Canada's economy);
- political (e.g., the *War Measures* Act effectively quelled the radical separatist movement in Quebec);

- educational (e.g., John A. Macdonald is not a good role model for students);
- environmental (e.g., industrialism was a disaster for the environment).

None of these are moral judgments because the person is not recommending (or condemning) the practices as ethically justifiable (or unjustifiable). The person could state without contradiction that despite the merits (or shortfalls), these practices should not (or should) have been pursued. For example, the person might believe that the human cost of free trade outweighs any economic benefit, or that despite Macdonald's failings it is still acceptable to teach students about him. Value judgments are moral judgments only when they assess whether, all things considered, an action or a conclusion is ethically responsible or justifiable.

Value judgments are often explicit but they may be implicit. Moral judgments and other kinds of value judgments are often present in historical accounts. These judgments can be explicit or implicit:

Explicit value judgment:	Life as a consumer is much better now than it was in pioneer times.
Implicit value judgment:	In pioneer times, people endured travel by foot over long distances to secure supplies in a tiny trading post with limited selection and uneven quality. Now we have the freedom to drive in temperature-controlled cars to our choice of malls where we find a wide selection of dependable goods.

Both these statement are evaluative—they are not simply describing conditions; they are passing judgment on the relative merits of pioneer and contemporary shopping. The explicit assessment is simply more obvious than the implied approval in the second account. The implicit approval becomes more obvious when we contrast it with an account by someone who does not endorse modern consumer practices:

Implicit (negative) value judgment:	Now we are addicted to environment-polluting vehicles that further isolate us from our surroundings as we race among a smorgasbord of malls offering excessive arrays of sanitized and largely unnecessary goods.

Encourage students to notice value-laden or non-neutral terminology indicating that an historical account is simply describing a state of affairs but are offering an evaluation of it, particularly when this is a moral judgment.

Moral judgments about the past must be sensitive to historical context. When reaching moral judgments about the past, we will inevitably draw upon contemporary values and norms. However, it would be unfair to overlook the historical context. We must not be indifferent to the values and conditions operating at the time. Many historical practices that people undertook with sincere intentions and in good conscience are no longer regarded as defensible. We may still want to condemn certain actions, but we cannot simply dismiss the beliefs and norms of the time. This sensitivity is apparent in our contemporary legal system when the courts show reluctance to impose laws retroactively (i.e., to hold someone legally responsible for an action completed before the law that made it illegal was enacted). So too, the courts may excuse or reduce the penalty for otherwise illegal actions if the conditions surrounding the action were exceptional (e.g., self-defence, euthanasia). In an analogous way, the actions that historical people took must be judged both in their own time and through contemporary standards. For example, the actions taken by the FLQ in 1970 may deserve a different moral judgment than would a contemporary group taking the same actions now. Quebec in the 1970's did not have a legitimate separatist party such as the Bloc Québécois or the Parti Québécois. The FLQ's actions need to be seen in that context—that there were no legitimate effective outlets for separatist feelings. This does not justify their actions but this information may cause us, to some extent, to look differently on the extreme measures they took.

There is value in withholding moral judgments until adequate information has been acquired. It is difficult to responsibly assign blame or credit to historical actions because we cannot know all the facts and we need, out of fairness, to be sensitive to the values and conditions of the time. Consequently, caution and, where possible, the suspension of judgment is advisable until the historical context has been explored. For example, while we might be inclined to condemn the loss of civil rights brought on by invoking the *War Measure Act*, we must be mindful that, at the time, no one knew how widespread the violence could grow. We might want to encourage students to withhold judgment until they appreciated the uncertain state of affairs in October 1970.

Determining cause is different from assigning responsibility. When judging an individual's moral responsibility for an historical event, students need to consider more than whether or not the person was a cause of the action. They need to consider who had obligations or power to affect the outcome (e.g., a child running into a street may be the cause of an action, but it might have been the parents' responsibility to ensure that the child was not in a position to do this). Similarly in history a particular individual might have delivered the abuse to Aboriginal students in residential schools, but an equal responsibility for these events may lie elsewhere, with those who ran the schools or who knew better and didn't do anything to prevent further abuse. Similarly, the kidnapping of James Cross and the murder of Pierre Laporté were immediate causes of the declaration of the *War Measures Act*, but the responsibility for the decision to declare it lay to a significant degree with Pierre Trudeau and his cabinet.

Introducing the concept to students

Before exploring moral judgments in various aspects of their study of history, it will be useful to help students recognize when historians are offering moral judgments and appreciate the need to consider the historical context before drawing any moral conclusions.

Recognizing judgments in historical accounts. Present students with an historical account from their textbook and invite them to distinguish the purely descriptive claims from those that are evaluative. Encourage students to look for implicit value judgments by noting evaluative or non-neutral terminology (e.g., "people put up with" rather than "people took part in"). In addition, help students distinguish those judgments that are moral or ethical in nature from those that are not. Rather than teaching the traditional "fact" versus "opinion" dichotomy, it would be clearer to distinguish factual (descriptive) statements from value statements (or statements of fact versus value judgments):

Factual claim:	Fur traders believed that selling liquor to First Nations people gave them an advantage in trade.
Non-moral value judgment:	If you wanted to gain the advantage in the fur trade, you would have been foolish not to sell liquor to First Nations people. [The author isn't making a moral judgment but rather a judgment on the economic effectiveness of the strategy.]
Moral judgment:	We shouldn't condemn fur traders for selling liquor to the First Nations people. They were simply doing what was necessary under the conditions and it wasn't their responsibility to look after the First Nations interests. [The author believes that fur traders were not to be blamed morally for selling liquor to the First Nations people.]

Considering historical context. One way to sensitize students to the need to consider context is to present a provocative historical quote, such as the first quote listed below, and invite students to react to it. After discussing their judgments, present other quotes from the same or different source in regards to the same event that contradict or mediate the message in the provocative quote (see example below). Invite students to reassess their original judgments in light of the additional information.

Initial quote by Mackenzie-King upon the dropping of the atom bomb on Hiroshima:

> *It is fortunate that the use of the bomb should have been upon the Japanese rather than upon the white races of Europe.*

Second quote by Mackenzie-King from the summer of 1945:

> *It makes one very sad at heart to think of the loss of life that it will occasion among innocent people as well as those that are guilty. It can only be justified through the knowledge that for one life destroyed, it may save hundreds of thousands and bring this terrible war quickly to a close.*

Third quote by US President Harry S Truman, 11 August 1945, in a letter justifying his decision to drop the atomic bomb on Hiroshima and Nagasaki:

> *The only language [the Japanese] seem to understand is the one we have been using to bombard them. When you have to deal with a beast you have to treat him as a beast. It is most regrettable but nevertheless true.*

Applications across the curriculum

Once students have an understanding of moral judgments, they can then consider this concept when thinking about historical events. Below are various ways in which it can be applied throughout the history curriculum.

Assessing accomplishments or actions. A common application of moral judgment is to invite students to ethically assess an historical individual or action (e.g., Was Simon Fraser a hero or a rogue? Was the decision to invoke the *War Measures Act* warranted?). When assessing moral judgments, emphasize the need to consider the values and practices of the times. Although students need not accept values from the past as our own, they must understand them and the context surrounding the actions and events.

Example: Ask students to imagine that they lived in 1920 before the Person's Case declared that women were legally persons and well before social values had changed to the point they had in 1968 when the divorce laws changed. Point out to the students that divorce laws prior to 1968 prevented married couples from obtaining a divorce on the grounds that they simply no longer wanted to be married. Couples were forced into manufacturing fictitious incidents of adultery or admitting to cruelty or desertion in order to obtain a divorce. Poll students and see how many would agree with the above provisions for divorce and how many would not. Elicit responses from those who would reject the laws. Then ask students to consider why such laws might have existed. Some reasons might include:

- Religious values of the time on the sanctity of marriage (especially Catholicism);
- The economic dependence of most women upon their husbands;
- The perception of women as the weaker sex that required protection.

Direct students to write an editorial as a person living in the 1920s either advocating for divorce reforms or retention of the divorce laws taking into account the values of the times. Provide background material to help students understand the differing historical perspectives.

Assigning moral responsibility. An important dimension of moral judgment involves assigning moral responsibility for actions people have taken or failed to take. When assigning responsibility we distinguish between individual and collective responsibility.

- ***Assessing the responsibility of historical figures***. Typically many individuals share responsibility for an historical event. Invite students to identify who is the most responsible or to assign degrees of responsibility to several individuals.

  Example: In 2000, the water supply in Walkerton, Ontario became infected by E. coli. Seven people died and hundreds became ill. It was later discovered the local official responsible for water quality, Stan Koebel, had lied, falsified records, failed to test water quality regularly, and when the outbreak occurred had failed to promptly notify the local Medical Officer of Health. A few years earlier, Premier Mike Harris's government had enacted "The Common Sense Revolution" which reduced the provincial deficit by drastically slashing funding for services and by cutting taxes. Many people argued that Harris' funding cuts had resulted in impaired inspection services, creating a situation in which Stan Koebel had been able to lie and falsify records.

  Direct students to set up a commission of inquiry to determine what portion, if any, of the blame for the Walkerton deaths is shared by each of the following: Mr. Koebel, Mr. Harris, the provincial cabinet, and any other individuals that students deem culpable.

- ***Assessing collective responsibility.*** Invite students to consider the collective responsibility that groups or institutions might share for an historic outcome. Although only individuals can initiate actions, often these actions could never have occurred were it not for the active or passive support of groups. For instance, one could blame Adolf Hitler solely for the Holocaust, but the magnitude of that genocide depended on the willingness of many individuals to carry it out and on the complicit approval of the citizens of Nazi Germany through their failure to oppose it. On the other hand, collective moral responsibility for the institution of slavery in the United States is more difficult to assign as there is ample evidence of active opposition to it within the United States even before it became a central cause of the Civil War.

Example: In January of 1942, after the Japanese bombing of Pearl Harbor, the Mackenzie-King government declared the coast of British Columbia a "protected area" and gave orders that every Japanese Canadian was to be removed from the area. The Japanese were moved to the BC interior despite the fact that the chief officer of the RCMP reported to intelligence experts that there "was no evidence of espionage or sabotage among the Japanese in BC [and]… As many of these people are Canadian citizens, we could not produce evidence necessary to justify our actions."[2] Assign students to take on the role of modern day Japanese Canadians who are direct descendants of the interned Japanese Canadians. They are to write a magazine article explaining who bears ultimate responsibility for the internment.

- ***Assessing the responsibility of current generations***. Another aspect of moral judgment involves deciding what responsibility, if any, current institutions or people living today have for the actions of past generations.

  Example: Ask students to role-play a Parliamentary Committee charged with establishing redress for the actions of the government in connection with residential schools. The committee will decide what, if any, compensation shall be paid to the actual victims or to their family for their pain and suffering. They will decide if a formal apology to Aboriginal peoples is necessary and if so what form such an apology should take. Students can read testimony from survivors as well as from government authorities from that period.

---

[2] From *At First A Dream: One Hundred Years of Race Relations in Vancouver,* produced by the Special Council Committee on Race Relations, Vancouver School Board, pp. 16-17.

Exemplar: Simon Fraser

8

In this chapter, we provide detailed activities and various primary and secondary sources to support six critical thinking tasks—one for each of the concepts discussed in this resource. All of these tasks focus on Simon Fraser's exploration of the Fraser River in 1808. For demonstration purposes, we have designed the activities as though every lesson was to be taught in the order in which it is presented. When using these lessons with a class, you may want to select from them and re-order them. However, when adapting these lessons, check that students will have all the tools they need to address the tasks presented to them.

Historical concept	Critical challenge
Significance	*What was the most significant event in Fraser's journey?*
Evidence	*Based on the additional sources, propose at least five revisions to the account of Fraser's journey to reflect your conclusion about the expedition.*
Continuity and change	*Construct a before and after profile of Fraser's character. To what extent did the journey change Fraser as a man?*
Historical perspective	*Why did various First Nations people respond to Fraser as they did in the three identified incidents? Retell one of the incidents from a First Nations perspective.*
Cause and consequence	*Based on their experiences with Fraser, how might Chief Whattlekainum and his people react to further visits from these "Sky-people"?*
Moral judgment	*How should Simon Fraser be remembered—more as a hero or a rogue?*

Introduce the culminating task

Set the context. Mention to students that Simon Fraser is a famous Canadian explorer—among other forms of recognition, a major river and a university have been named after him. Display the C.W. Jeffery's drawing *Simon Fraser Descending the Fraser River, 1808* (Blackline Master #11) on an overhead transparency and use *Map of the Fraser River* (Blackline Master #12) to trace Fraser's route. Indicate that in 1808, Fraser traveled by water and over land for approximately 800 kilometers on his roundtrip from Fort George (now Prince George, British Columbia) to what is now New Westminster. Suggest that there is some reason to suspect that history has been too kind to Fraser—that he may or may not deserve his acclaim. The ultimate point of the activities is to determine exactly what contemporary reputation or legacy Simon Fraser deserves. Before doing that, students must learn the facts of his journey and think though a number of critical tasks.

Critical task #1 – Significance

Introduce the first critical challenge. Invite students to imagine they have been asked to select a single scene for use in creating an Heritage Minute capturing a significant incident during Fraser's journey in 1808. Explain that their critical thinking task is to decide the following question:

> *What was the most significant event in Fraser's journey?*

Introduce criteria for significance. Explain or review the following (or other) criteria for determining historical significance:

- Was *prominent* at the time (Was it a noticeable event then?);
- Had notable *consequences* (Did it affect the rest of the trip and beyond the trip?);
- Influenced *subsequent profile* (Is it memorable or revealing about Fraser?).

If students have not worked with these criteria, invite them to identify several significant events in their own lives and explain if and how each criterion applies. You may want to use the chart *Comparing significance* (Blackline Master #1) to structure this task. Ask students to list the events in order of significance and to explain their ranking. The assessment rubric found in *Assessing the rankings* (Blackline Master #13) may be used to provide feedback to students.

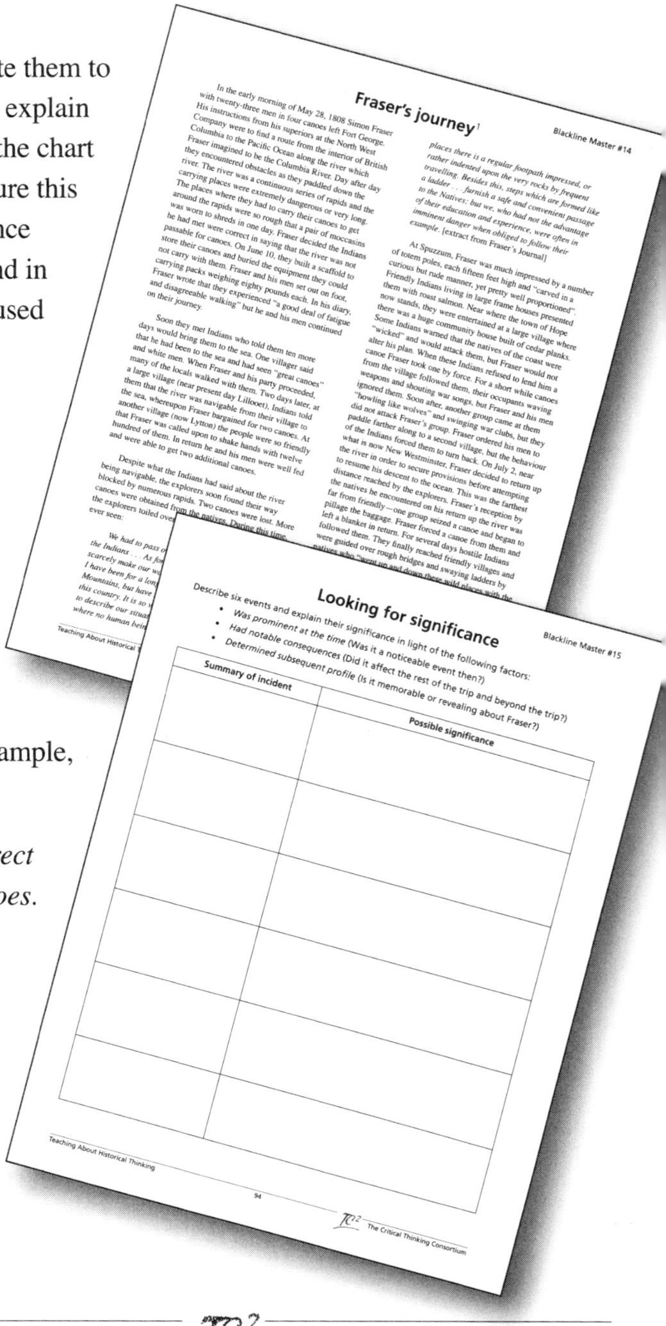

Look for significant incidents. Distribute the briefing sheet *Fraser's journey* (Blackline Master #14). As students work in small groups to read the briefing sheet, ask them to circle or underline any events that may be significant about Simon Fraser's journey. When finished this task, students are to summarize six incidents on the chart *Looking for significance* (Blackline Master #15) and explain each event's significance, referring to the appropriate criteria. For example, in the first paragraph, the briefing sheet states:

> *Fraser decided the Indians he had met were correct in saying that the river was not passable for canoes. On June 10, they built a scaffold to store their canoes and buried the equipment they could not carry with them. Fraser and his men set out on foot, carrying packs weighing eighty pounds each.*

This statement might be recorded as follows.

Summary of incident	Possible significance
Fraser decides to leave canoes and equipment behind and to proceed on foot.	• *Very little prominence at the time, although he may have agonized over the decision;* • *Notable consequences: for the rest of his journey, Fraser would be dependent on First Nations people for any further canoes.* • *Revealing: shows Fraser's willingness to heed the advice of First Nations people.*

Select the most significant incident. Once students have identified six incidents, each group is to select one or two that appear more significant than the rest and prepare a brief justification. Discuss each group's recommendations and try to reach consensus as a class on three candidates for the most significant event of Fraser's journey. Individually, students are to assess and rank order each of the short-listed events. You may want to use the chart in Blackline Master #1 to structure this task and the rubric in Blackline Master #13 to assess student responses. Ask students to write a paragraph explaining which event is most significant, considering its intended use in a Heritage Minute.

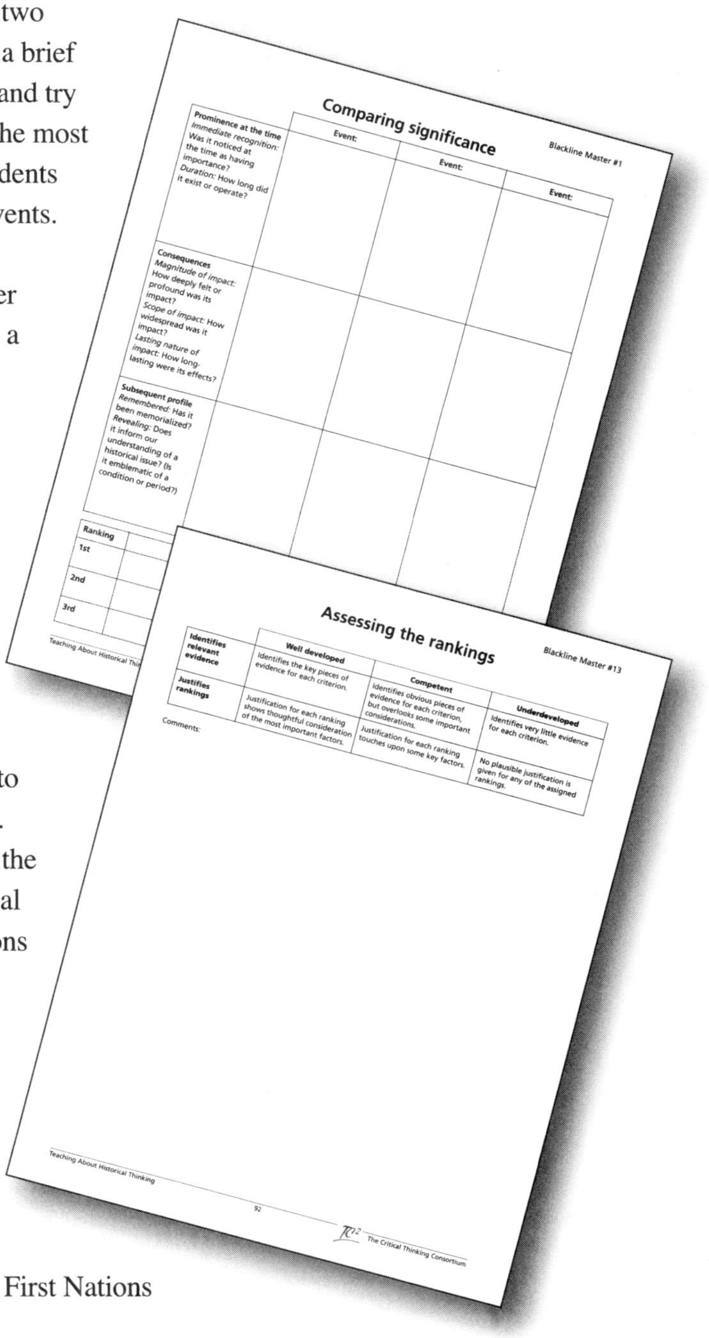
Comparing significance

Blackline Master #1

	Event:	Event:	Event:
Prominence at the time *Immediate recognition:* Was it noticed at the time as having importance? *Duration:* How long did it exist or operate?			
Consequences *Magnitude of impact:* How deeply felt or profound was its impact? *Scope of impact:* How widespread was its impact? *Lasting nature of impact:* How long-lasting were its effects?			
Subsequent profile *Remembered:* Has it been memorialized? *Revealing:* Does it inform our understanding of a historical issue? (Is it emblematic of a condition or period?)			

Ranking	
1st	
2nd	
3rd	

Teaching About Historical Thinking

Assessing the rankings

Blackline Master #13

	Well developed	Competent	Underdeveloped
Identifies relevant evidence	Identifies the key pieces of evidence for each criterion.	Identifies obvious pieces of evidence for each criterion, but overlooks some important considerations.	Identifies very little evidence for each criterion.
Justifies rankings	Justification for each ranking shows thoughtful consideration of the most important factors.	Justification for each ranking touches upon some key factors.	No plausible justification is given for any of the assigned rankings.

Comments:

Teaching About Historical Thinking 92 The Critical Thinking Consortium

Critical task #2 – Evidence

Discuss theories about Fraser's journey. Explain to the students that historians do more than present facts; they construct historical narratives that explain events. When historians use information to support an historical conclusion, it becomes evidence. This means any particular piece of information about the past becomes evidence only in response to an historical theory or issue. Brainstorm possible overall conclusions that explain how Fraser was able to complete his exploration of the river. These may include:

- Simon Fraser was successful in his journey because he was able to depend on First Nations peoples for food, directions and support.
- Simon Fraser relied more on his skills of diplomacy than force to get the cooperation of First Nations peoples.

- Simon Fraser's arrogance, assertiveness and self-assuredness got him down the river that bears his name.
- It was a very dangerous mission and Fraser was lucky to return home without injury to self or others.

Present the additional sources. Draw students' attention to the fact that they have derived their knowledge of Fraser's trip exclusively from one secondary account (Blackline Master #14). Discuss the problems of doing this (e.g., limited facts, difficult to tell if the account is accurate, may represent only one perspective). After a short discussion, distribute three additional sources:

- selected excerpts from Fraser's diaries (Blackline Master #16),
- a primary account by Jules Quesnel, one of Fraser's lieutenants on this trip (Blackline Master #17)
- a secondary 20th century textbook account by Tony Cashman (Blackline Master #18).

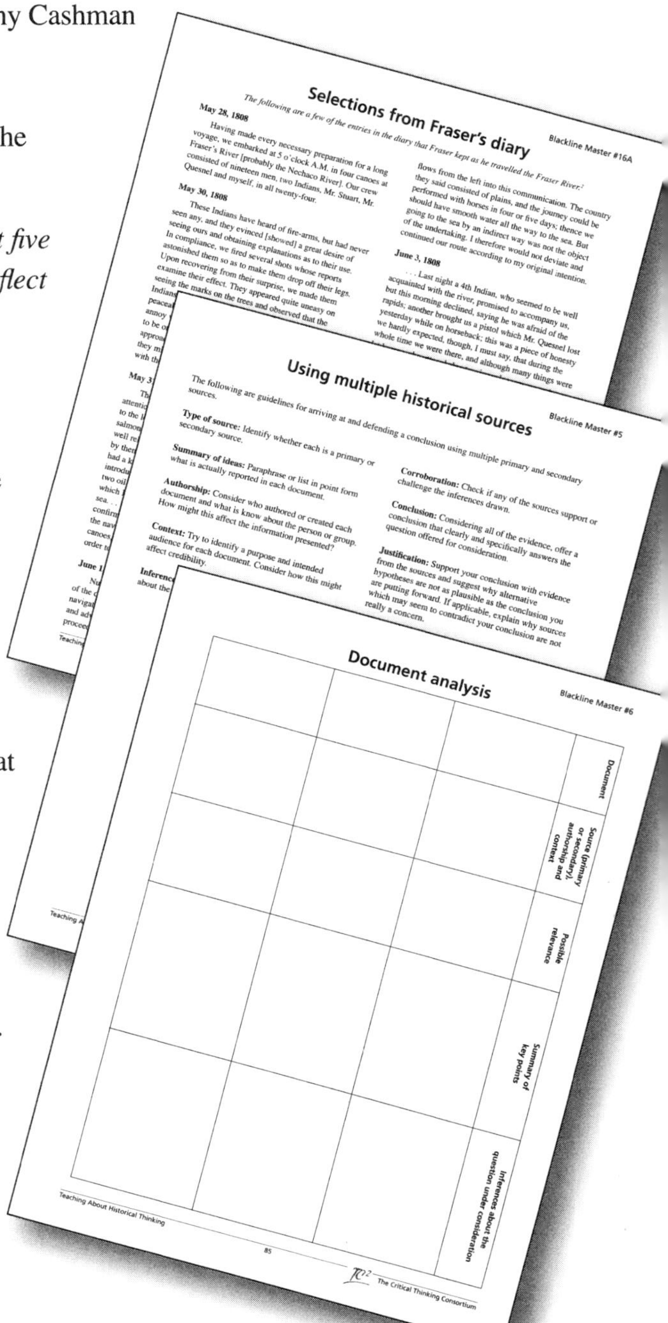

Introduce the second critical challenge. Explain that the students' next critical thinking task is as follows:

> *Based on the additional sources, propose at least five revisions to the account of Fraser's journey to reflect your conclusion about the expedition.*

Explain that students will be expected to read the additional sources, decide on a conclusion that is supported by the evidence and then propose at least five changes to the initial account of the journey presented in Blackline Master #14.

Analyze the additional sources. To support students in their analysis of the additional resources, review the following guidelines found in *Using multiple historical sources* (Blackline Master #5) and suggest that students use the chart in *Document analysis* (Blackline Master #6) to record their ideas:

- *Type of source*: Identify whether each is a primary or secondary source.
- *Summary of ideas*: Paraphrase or list in point form what is actually reported in each document.
- *Authorship*: Consider who authored or created each document and what is known about the person or group. How might this affect the information presented?
- *Context*: Try to identify a purpose and an intended audience for each document. Consider how this might affect credibility.

- *Inferences*: Look to draw inferences from each source about the question you are trying to answer.
- *Corroboration*: Check if any of the sources support or challenge the inferences drawn.
- *Conclusion*: Considering all of the evidence, offer a conclusion that clearly and specifically answers the question offered for consideration.
- *Justification*: Support your conclusion with evidence from the sources and suggest why alternative hypotheses are not as plausible as the conclusion you are putting forward. If applicable, explain why sources that may seem to contradict your conclusion are not really a problem.

Look for corroborating or contradictory evidence. After students have completed a preliminary analysis of the three additional sources encourage them to look for corroboration and inconsistencies between these and the initial account. As an example, draw students' attention to the discrepancies in the reported number of people on the trip:

- Quesnel states: *Now I must tell you that I went exploring this summer with Mr. Simon Fraser and John Stuart, whom I believe you know. We were accompanied by 12 men in three canoes.*
- Fraser's diary for May 22, 1808 offers a different number: *Having made every necessary preparation for a long voyage, we embarked at 5 o'clock A.M. in four canoes at Fraser's River. Our crew consisted of nineteen men, two Indians, Mr. Stuart, Mr. Quesnel and myself, in all twenty-four.*
- Cashman's account is different yet again: *On May 22 Fraser and eight men left Fort Fraser to ride the Columbia to its mouth.*

Discuss how such confusion could occur over what seems to be a straightforward piece of information. Which account should be believed? Invite students to suggest which source overall seems most credible and why.

Propose their recommendations. Direct students in groups to propose approximately six additions or changes to the account provided in Blackline Master #14 that makes the account more accurate and supports students' conclusions about Fraser's journey. You may want students to use the chart *Revising the account* (Blackline Master #19) to identify their proposed changes in the left-hand column and record their evidence for these recommendations in the right-hand column. Arrange for students to share their recommendations.

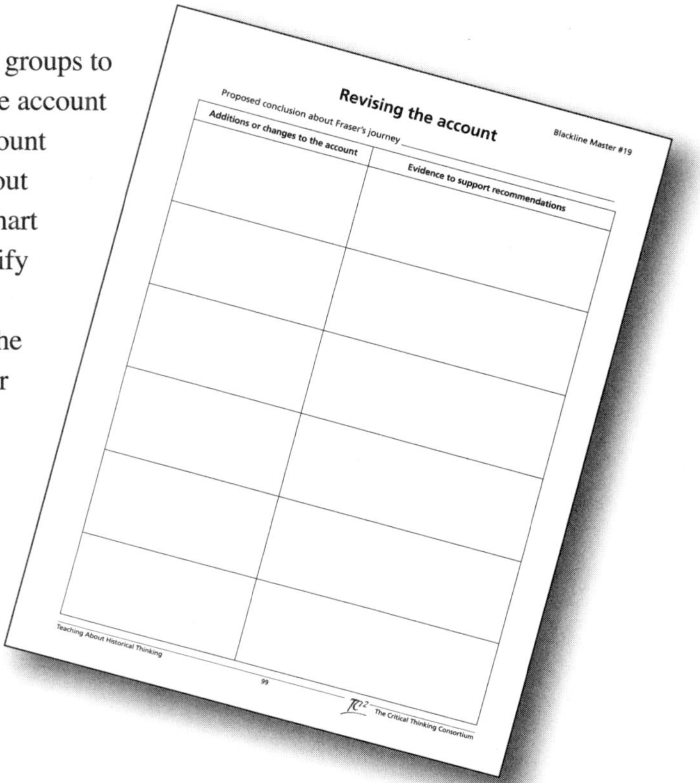
Blackline Master #19

Revising the account

Proposed conclusion about Fraser's journey

Additions or changes to the account	Evidence to support recommendations

Teaching About Historical Thinking 99 TC² The Critical Thinking Consortium

Critical task #3 - Continuity and change

Introduce the third critical challenge. Suggest to students that difficult journeys such as the one Fraser undertook might change a person in profound ways (e.g., people who climb Mount Everest or astronauts who travel to the Moon have found the experiences life altering). Given the physical and emotional challenges that Fraser faced, what type of changes might he have undergone as a man? Explain to students that the first part of their next task is as follows:

> *Construct a before and after profile of Fraser's character.*

Construct start-of-trip profile. Organize students in groups to identify at least five traits that characterize Fraser as the beginning of his journey. Students may use evidence from the opening descriptions of any of the sources and also from subsequent comments that implied he was changed by certain occurrences. Distribute copies of the chart *Before and after profiles* (Blackline Master #20) for students to record the traits at the start of the trip and their evidence for attributing these traits to Fraser. Encourage students to provide more than one piece of evidence for each trait. You may want to use the rubric found in *Assessing character traits* (Blackline Master #21) to provide students with feedback on their responses. Invite groups to share and discuss their finding with the class.

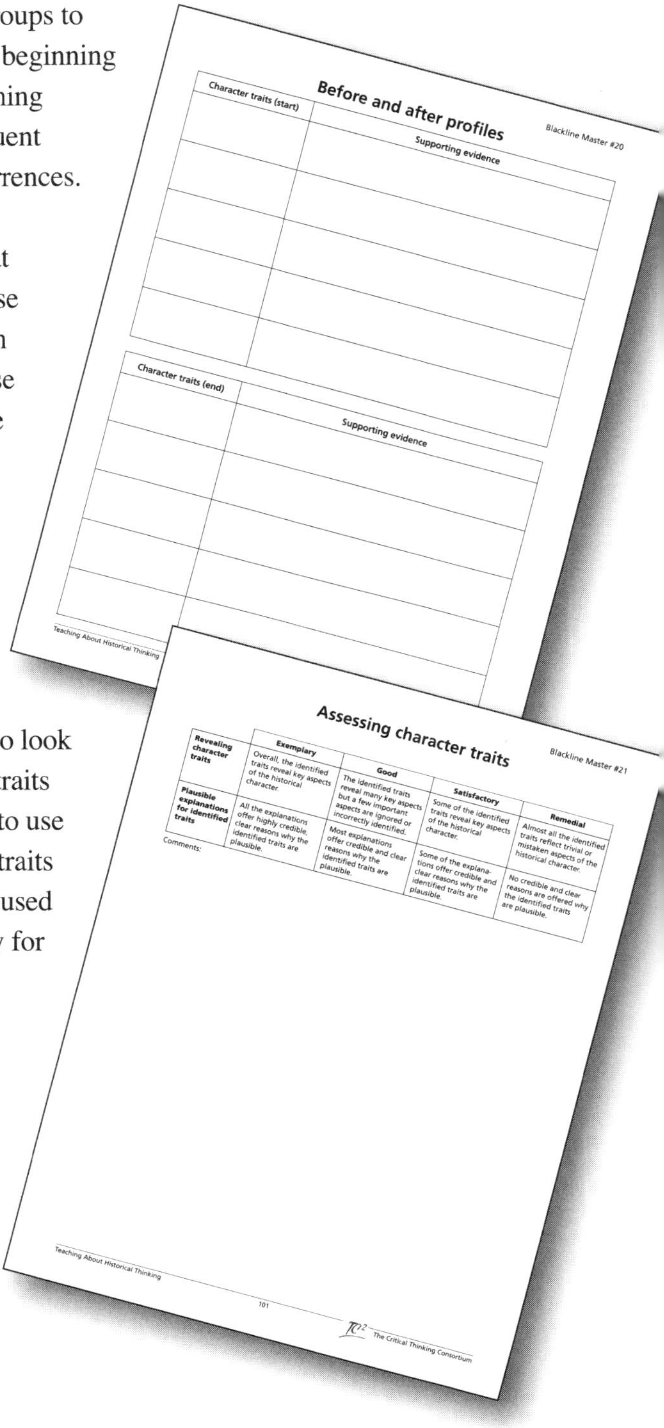

Construct end-of-trip profile. When students have shared and, if desired, revised their profile of Fraser at the start of his journey, direct each group to develop an end-of-journey profile. Encourage students to look for differences in Fraser, but also to note where certain traits have continued throughout the journey. Direct students to use the bottom half of Blackline Master #20 to record their traits and supporting evidence. Blackline Master #21 may be used to assess these responses. Again, provide an opportunity for students to share their findings with others in the class.

Present the concluding task. Explain to students that their concluding task in this lesson is to address the following question:

> *To what extent did the journey change Fraser as a man?*

Based on their comparative profiles invite students to prepare a one-page answer to this question. Direct students to provide a clear conclusion about the extent of change in Fraser (e.g., greatly changed, hardly changed at all) and to explain with reference to specific evidence why they have reached this conclusion and not other conclusions. You may want to use the chart *Justifying my conclusion* (Blackline Master #22) to structure this activity and the rubric found in *Assessing the justification* (Blackline Master #23) to assess student responses.

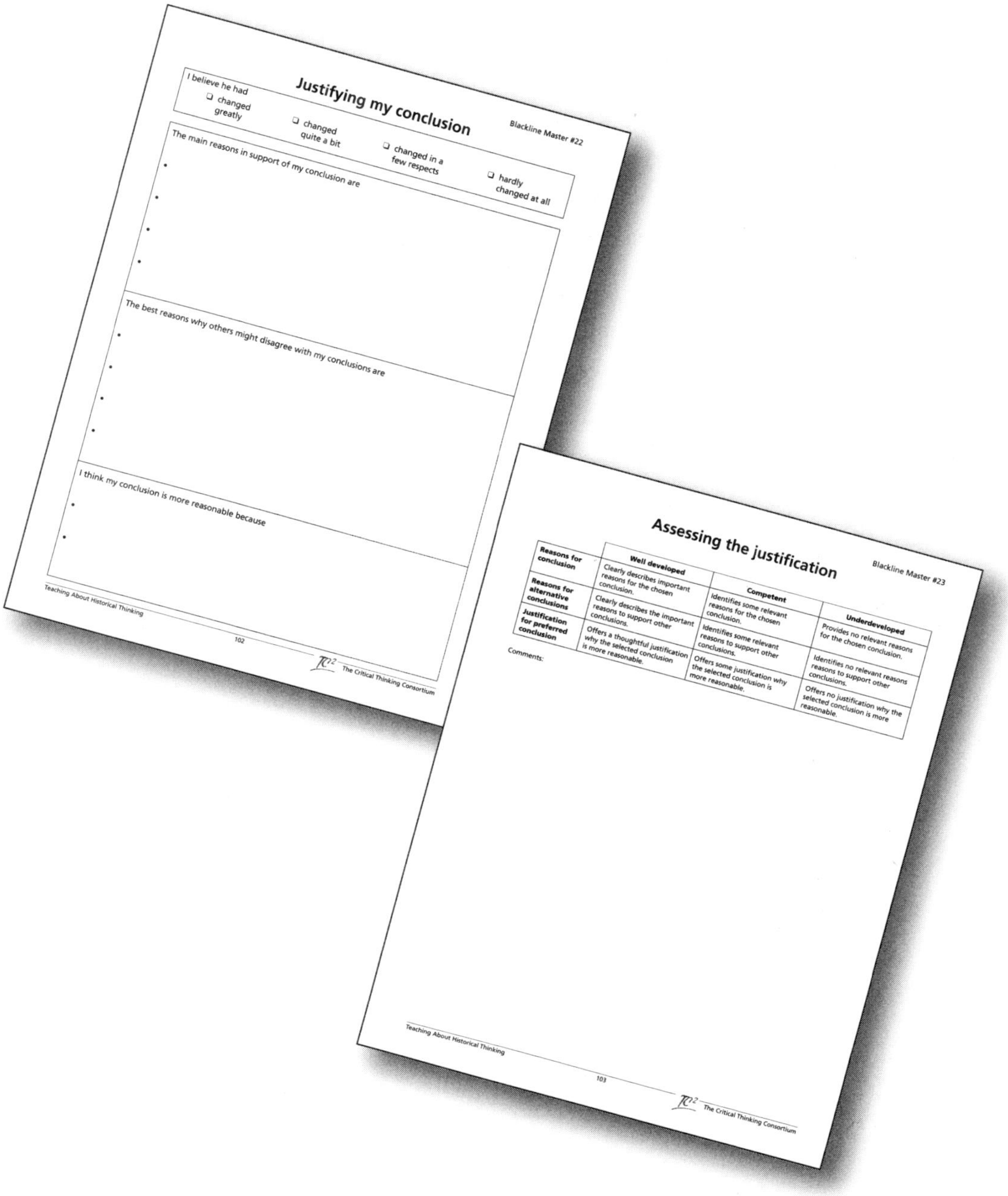
Justifying my conclusion

Blackline Master #22

I believe he had

❑ changed greatly ❑ changed quite a bit ❑ changed in a few respects ❑ hardly changed at all

The main reasons in support of my conclusion are

The best reasons why others might disagree with my conclusions are

I think my conclusion is more reasonable because

Teaching About Historical Thinking 102 The Critical Thinking Consortium

Assessing the justification

Blackline Master #23

	Well developed	Competent	Underdeveloped
Reasons for conclusion	Clearly describes important reasons for the chosen conclusion.	Identifies some relevant reasons for the chosen conclusion.	Provides no relevant reasons for the chosen conclusion.
Reasons for alternative conclusions	Clearly describes the important reasons to support other conclusions.	Identifies some relevant reasons to support other conclusions.	Identifies no relevant reasons to support other conclusions.
Justification for preferred conclusion	Offers a thoughtful justification why the selected conclusion is more reasonable.	Offers some justification why the selected conclusion is more reasonable.	Offers no justification why the selected conclusion is more reasonable.

Comments:

Teaching About Historical Thinking 103 The Critical Thinking Consortium

Critical task #4 - Historical perspective

Introduce the fourth critical challenge. Remind students that when studying about historical events, we want to understand why people (as individuals and groups) acted as they did. To do this we must learn about their motivations or intentions, and also about the circumstances, cultural beliefs and societal values that would likely have influenced them. Select three events from any of the accounts of Fraser's journey. These might include the following:

- twelve hundred members of a First Nations community (at what is now Lytton) shook Fraser's hand;
- First Nations people (near what is now Hope) refused to lend him a canoe;
- First Nations people in canoes shouted and swung their clubs but did not attack Fraser's group.

Present students with the following question:

Why did various First Nations peoples respond to Fraser as they did in the three identified incidents?

Brainstorm possible explanations. As a class or in groups, invite students to speculate about possible reasons for the behaviour of the First Nations people in the three incidents (e.g., perhaps their motivation for shaking hands was friendship, politeness, curiousity, or deference to strangers). Encourage students to be as specific as possible (e.g., instead of saying simply the First Nations people wanted to be friendly, explain what might evoke this desire). Direct students to look to broader economic, cultural, and religious factors to explain why they acted in these ways. Invite students to identify evidence that might support each proposed explanation. You may want students to use the chart found in *Explaining their actions* (Blackline Master #24) to structure this activity.

Introduce a First Nations account. Draw students' attention to the fact that all of the sources of information about Fraser's trip have been by people of European ancestry. Assign students, in pairs, to read the view of Fraser's trip found in *A First Nations account* (Blackline Master #25). Encourage students to consult other First Nations' sources on this expedition. Direct students to use this information to supplement and revise evidence they have accumulated thus far.

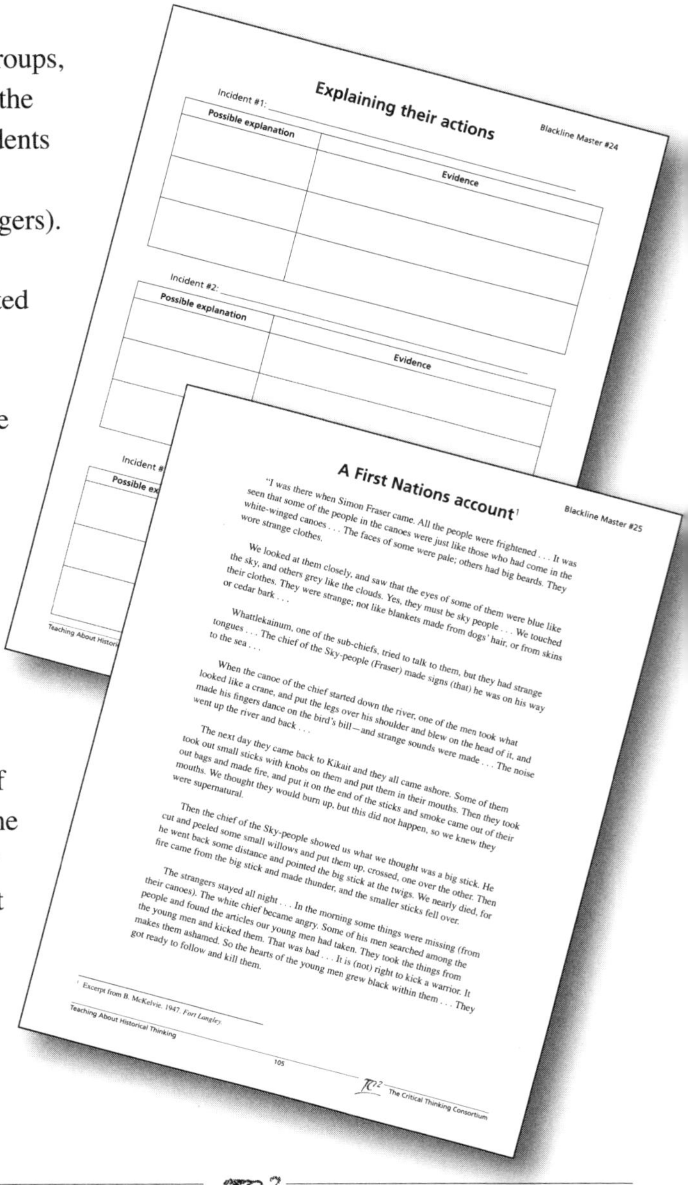
Explaining their actions

Blackline Master #24

Incident #1:

Possible explanation	Evidence

Incident #2:

Possible explanation	Evidence

Incident #3:

Teaching About Historical Thinking

A First Nations account[1]

Blackline Master #25

"I was there when Simon Fraser came. All the people were frightened . . . It was seen that some of the people in the canoes were just like those who had come in the white-winged canoes . . . The faces of some were pale; others had big beards. They wore strange clothes.

We looked at them closely, and saw that the eyes of some of them were blue like the sky, and others grey like the clouds. Yes, they must be sky people . . . We touched their clothes. They were strange; not like blankets made from dogs' hair, or from skins or cedar bark . . .

Whattlekainum, one of the sub-chiefs, tried to talk to them, but they had strange tongues . . . The chief of the Sky-people (Fraser) made signs (that) he was on his way to the sea . . .

When the canoe of the chief started down the river, one of the men took what looked like a crane, and put the legs over his shoulder and blew on the head of it, and made his fingers dance on the bird's bill—and strange sounds were made . . . The noise went up the river and back . . .

The next day they came back to Kikait and they all came ashore. Some of them took out small sticks with knobs on them and put them in their mouths. Then they took out bags and made fire, and put it on the end of the sticks and smoke came out of their mouths. We thought they would burn up, but this did not happen, so we knew they were supernatural.

Then the chief of the Sky-people showed us what we thought was a big stick. He cut and peeled some small willows and put them up, crossed, one over the other. Then he went back some distance and pointed the big stick at the twigs. We nearly died, for fire came from the big stick and made thunder, and the smaller sticks fell over.

The strangers stayed all night . . . In the morning some things were missing (from their canoes). The white chief became angry. Some of his men searched among the people and found the articles our young men had taken. They took the things from the young men and kicked them. That was bad . . . It is (not) right to kick a warrior. It makes them ashamed. So the hearts of the young men grew black within them . . . They got ready to follow and kill them.

[1] Excerpt from B. McKelvie. 1947. *Fort Langley*.

Teaching About Historical Thinking 105 The Critical Thinking Consortium

Decide on the most plausible explanation. After accumulating evidence to support each explanation, invite students to determine the major motivation or factor that explains why the First Nations people acted as they did in each of the three identified incidents. Remind students that their proposed major influence must be supported by the historical evidence and must plausibly be seen to be more influential than other factors. Ask students to write a paragraph for each incident where they justify their conclusion in light of these two criteria.

Rewrite a First Nations perspective. Introduce the final task in this lesson:

> *Retell one of the incidents from a First Nations perspective.*

Ask students to select one of these incidents and describe in detail that encounter from a First Nation's perspective explaining the actions that First Nation took and why? Encourage students to consider the following criteria when developing their account:

- consistency with the accepted facts;
- plausible given what is known generally about the people and the time;
- offers specific insight into the worldview of the First Nations people represented.

Critical task #5 - Cause and consequence

Introduce the fifth critical challenge. In a previous briefing sheet (Blackline Master #25), students read descriptions of *Chief Whattlekainum's* and his people's perspectives on their interactions with Fraser and his men. Using this a starting point, invite students to consider the following question:

> *Based on their experiences with Fraser, how might Chief Whattlekainum and his people react to further visits from these "Sky-people"?*

Brainstorm possible effects. As a class or in groups, invite students to speculate about possible effects of their initial encounter on First Nations people's attitudes to Europeans, Encourage students to be as specific as possible about likely consequences. Direct students to look to broader factors (e.g., social, economic, religious factors) that explain why it might produce this effect. Invite students to identify supporting evidence for each predicted reaction to a subsequent visit by Europeans.

Decide on the most likely consequence. After accumulating evidence to support each scenario, invite students to determine the most likely response of First Nations people to subsequent visits. Ask students to write a paragraph justifying their anticipated scenario in light of two criteria:

- is consistent with the accepted facts;
- plausible given what is known generally about the people and the time.

Critical task #6 - Moral judgment

Introduce the culminating critical challenge. Introduce the final critical thinking question:

> *How should Simon Fraser be remembered—more as a hero or a rogue?*

Explain that this question invites students to use all of the information and insight accumulated in the previous activities to develop a position on how Fraser deserves to be remembered in history. Does he warrant the honours that have been bestowed upon him? Students' overall judgment should take into account varying perspectives including Simon Fraser's, First Nations' perspectives, and our perspective on his lasting accomplishments and shortcomings.

Introduce the criteria for judgment. Discuss with students the criteria to consider when formulating their assessment of Fraser:

- core values we currently admire in leaders and heroes;
- values that may have been operating in the historical period.

To help students think about of these criteria, briefly discuss the following questions:

- As a person of his time, what kind of assessment would we offer?
- Exclusively considering current standards, how admirable do his actions appear today?

Introduce the task. Announce to students that they will be expected to explain their position by participating in a *U-shaped discussion*. This strategy offers an alternative to the traditional two-sided debate. Instead of an adversarial either/or format, students are encouraged to formulate a position along a continuum from great hero to shameless rogue. Allow time for students to develop a precise position on the reputation that Fraser deserves. You may want to invite students to use *Self-assessment of discussion* (Blackline Master #26) to help them prepare for the discussion.

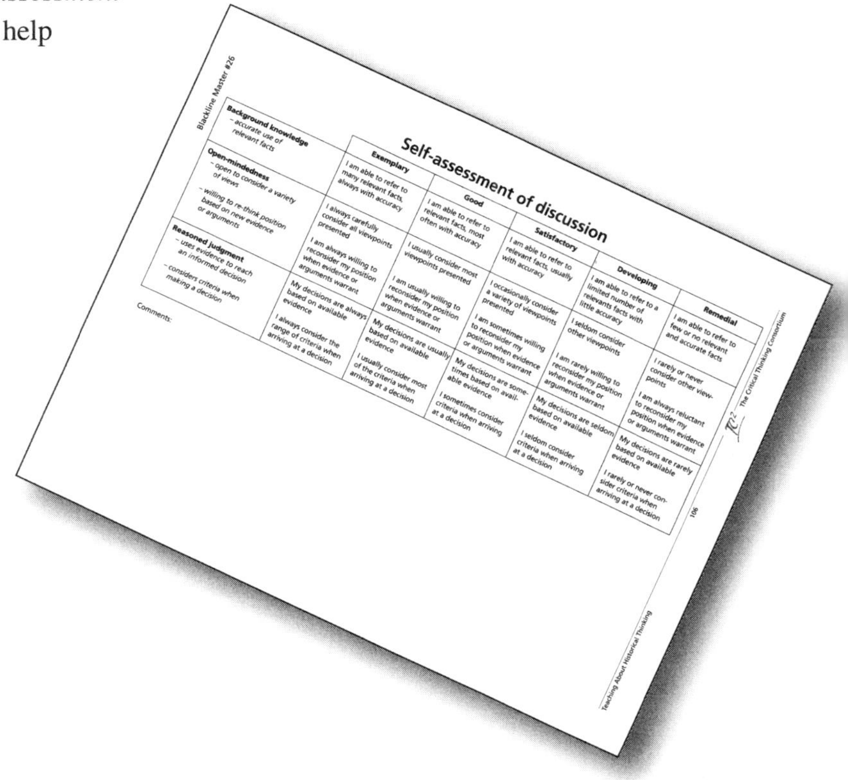
Blackline Master #26

Self-assessment of discussion

	Exemplary	Good	Satisfactory	Developing	Remedial
Background knowledge – accurate use of relevant facts	I am able to refer to many relevant facts, always with accuracy	I am able to refer to relevant facts, most often with accuracy	I am able to refer to relevant facts, usually with accuracy	I am able to refer to a limited number of relevants facts with little accuracy	I am able to refer to few or no relevant and accurate facts
Open-mindedness – open to consider a variety of views	I always carefully consider all viewpoints presented	I usually consider most viewpoints presented	I occasionally consider a variety of viewpoints presented	I seldom consider other viewpoints	I rarely or never consider other viewpoints
– willing to re-think position based on new evidence or arguments	I am always willing to reconsider my position when evidence or arguments warrant	I am usually willing to reconsider my position when evidence or arguments warrant	I am sometimes willing to reconsider my position when evidence or arguments warrant	I am rarely willing to reconsider my position when evidence or arguments warrant	I am always reluctant to reconsider my position when evidence or arguments warrant
Reasoned judgment – uses evidence to reach an informed decision	My decisions are always based on available evidence	My decisions are usually based on available evidence	My decisions are sometimes based on available evidence	My decisions are seldom based on available evidence	My decisions are rarely based on available evidence
– considers criteria when making a decision	I always consider the range of criteria when arriving at a decision	I usually consider most of the criteria when arriving at a decision	I sometimes consider criteria when arriving at a decision	I seldom consider criteria when arriving at a decision	I rarely or never consider criteria when arriving at a decision

Comments:

TC² The Critical Thinking Consortium 106 Teaching About Historical Thinking

Hold the U-shaped discussion. Arrange the class in a "U-shape." Students with polar views (either strongly endorsing Fraser or very critical of Fraser) seat themselves at either tip of the "U"; students with mixed opinions sit at appropriate spots along the rounded part. Begin by asking students at each tip of the "U" to state their position and offer a few reasons only. If there is an imbalance in strong support for one side or the other, locate yourself (temporarily) in a polar position to get the discussion going. Alternate from side to side, as students from all parts of the "U" offer their views. Stress that students are not to try to convince others, but to explain why the position they are sitting in is the most defensible one for them. At several stages in the discussion, encourage students to physically move along the spectrum if they have heard reasons that cause them to shift their intellectual position on the issue. The goal of the "U-shaped" discussion is to encourage students to endorse positions provisionally and to listen to others in an attempt to figure out the most defensible personal stance along a continuum of possibilities. Invite students to use Blackline Master #26 to self-assess their performance, and you may want to use *Assessing U-shaped discussion* (Blackline Master #27) to assess this activity.

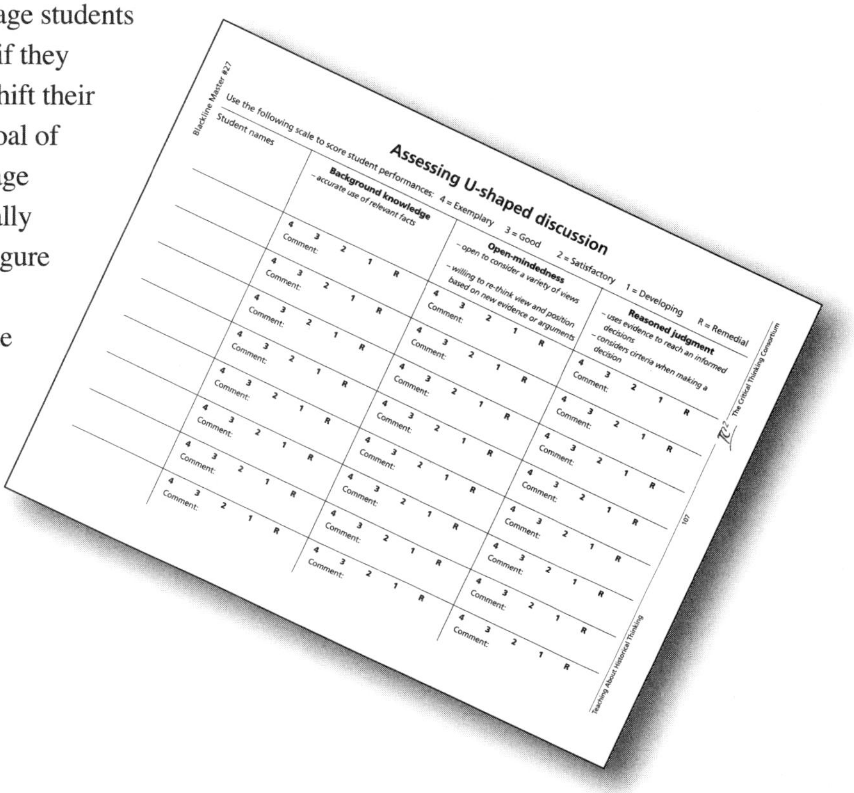

Concluding essay. If desired, direct students to prepare a short essay justifying their precise position on the issue. Encourage students to address possible counter-arguments that they may have encountered during the U-shaped discussion.

Extension

Apply to other explorers. Use some of the activities suggested here to guide students' inquiries into other Canadian explorers. Assign groups of students to research and assess the achievements of a particular explorer both from the explorer's perspective and from the perspective of those who traveled with or encountered the explorer. Each group is to share its findings with the rest of the class which then considers who was the most admirable Canadian explorer.

The connection between critical and historical thinking

9

In many curriculum documents, critical thinking is distinguished from other kinds of thinking, including from historical and geographic thinking. These divisions between thinking within a subject area and thinking critically are rather arbitrary and, in some respects, unhelpful. Is there really a difference between "thinking critically about an historical question" and "engaging in historical thinking"? What would it mean to engage in historical thinking if the person was not to think critically about sources, evidence, inferences, and conclusions. We believe that thinking critically is not divorced from thinking in history; on the contrary, critical thinking is closely aligned with sound thinking in history. The purpose of the chapter is to explore the interconnection between critical and historical thinking, particularly in the context of the model developed by The Critical Thinking Consortium.

Thinking critically about history

We believe critical thinking involves thinking through problematic situations about what to believe or how to act where the thinker makes reasoned judgments that embody the qualities of a competent thinker.

According to this definition, a person is attempting to think critically when she thoughtfully seeks to assess or judge what would be sensible or reasonable to believe or do in a given situation. Clearly, the need to reach reasoned judgments arises in countless kinds of problematic situations including the myriads of issues in history that have been discussed in previous chapters:

- Which of several events is the most significant?
- What was the real cause of this event?
- What would have happened if the result had turned out differently?
- Was the historical leader justified in the actions she took?
- What was it really like to live in this historical period?

All of these are problematic situations because there is some doubt as to the most appropriate conclusion. Each situation requires that we think critically about the options as there is no point in reaching a decision that is not sensible or reasonable. While it makes sense to distinguish thinking in history from thinking in geography—they differ in content and methods or inquiry—the same cannot be said for critical and historical thinking. In our view, thinking critically is a way of engaging in historical thinking, just as being careful is a way of walking down the stairs. In fact, we suggest there are only two ways of undertaking historical thinking: either in *a critically thoughtful way*—where the person attempts in matters historical to makes reasoned judgments that embody the qualities of a competent thinker—or in *a thoughtless way*—where the person doesn't care about having accurate historical information, reaching sound conclusions, being open to alterative viewpoints, and so on. Seen this way, thinking critically is not a unique *type* of thinking different from historical thinking, rather it refers to the *qualities* evident in good historical thinking.

Our emphasis in thinking critically is on the qualities that student responses should exhibit (e.g., accurate information, sound conclusions, open-minded). The challenge for history teachers is to identify and promote in their students the qualities that are especially relevant to thinking historically. This series, called *Tools for Historical Understanding*, is devoted to serving this very purpose. As we will see later in this chapter, this means developing the intellectual resources or "tools" that good historical thinkers requires.

Thinking critically about history will not be identical with thinking critically in geography because some of the requisite tools will differ. Students will need different *background knowledge*—they will need to access bodies of historical facts rather than geographic facts. The core concepts (or *critical thinking vocabulary*) in historical thinking—continuity and change, historical perspective, historical significance, cause and consequences, moral judgment—will differ to a large extent from those in geography, which focus on space, place and systems. In other respects, the tools will apply across disciplines: there will be commonalities in many of the *criteria for making reasoned judgments* (e.g., Is the source reliable? the evidence relevant? the conclusion warranted?) and in many of the *thinking strategies* that help students work though various issues (e.g., looking for connections, using graphic organizers to represent information, role playing various perspectives). The final type of tool, *habits of mind*, refers to attitudes such as open-minded, curiosity and an inquiring spirit that are shared very broadly across most forms of thinking.

To conclude this discussion, we believe that differences in the so-called forms of thinking can be explained by the overlapping constellation of "tools" that good critical thinkers in each of these subject areas or disciplines will require.

Promoting historical thinking through critical thinking

In our work with teachers in history (and in other subjects), we propose a four-pronged approach to enhance students' abilities to think critically:

- build a *community of thinkers* within the school and classroom;
- infuse opportunities for critical thinking—what we call *critical challenges*—throughout the curriculum;
- develop the *intellectual tools* that will enable students to become competent critical thinkers;
- on a continuing basis *assess students' competence* in using the intellectual tools to think through critical challenges.

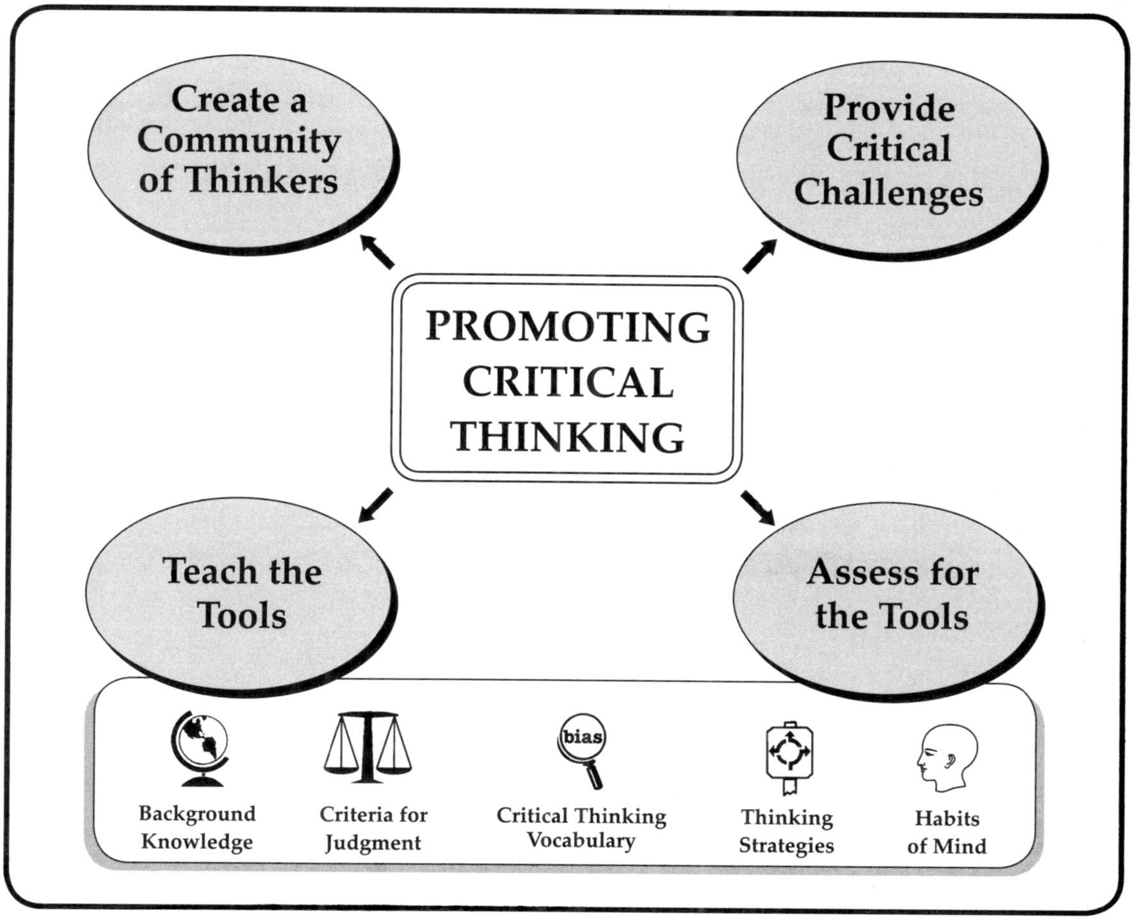

Building a community of thinkers

Developing supportive school and classroom communities where reflective inquiry is valued may be the most important factor in nurturing critical thinking. Student will not master the "tools" of critical thinking unless their use is reinforced on an ongoing basis. As well, the image of the thinker as a solitary figure is misleading. No one person can perfectly embody all the desired attributes—we must learn to rely on others to complement our own thoughts. There are many routines and norms that teachers can adopt to create a community of thinkers:

- Regularly pose questions and assignments requiring students to think through, and not merely recall, what is being learned.
- Creating ongoing opportunities to engage in critical and cooperative dialogue—confer, inquire, debate and critique—is key to creating a community of thinkers.
- Employ self- and peer-assessment as ways of involving students in thinking critically about their own work.
- Model good critical thinking practices. Students are more likely to learn to act in desired ways if they see teachers making every effort to be open-minded, to seek clarification where needed, to avoid reaching conclusions based on inadequate evidence, and so on.

Infusing critical challenges throughout the curriculum

If students are to improve their ability to think critically, they must have numerous opportunities to engage and think through problematic situations—what we refer to as *critical challenges.*

- *Does the question or task require judgment?* A question or task is a critical challenge only if it invites students to assess the reasonableness of plausible options or alternative conclusions. In short, it must require more than retrieval of information, rote application of a strategy, uninformed guessing or mere assertion of a preference.
- *Will the challenge be meaningful to students?* Trivial, decontextualized mental exercises often alienate or bore students. It is important to frame challenges that are likely to engage students in tackling questions and tasks that they will find meaningful.
- *Does the challenge address key aspects of the subject matter?* Critical thinking should not be divorced from the rest of the curriculum. Students are more likely to learn the content of the curriculum if they are invited to think critically about issues embedded in the subject matter.
- *Do students have the tools or can they reasonably acquire the tools needed to competently address the challenge?* Students need support in acquiring the essential tools required to competently meet the critical challenge.

Developing intellectual tools for thinking critically

As suggested earlier, the key to helping students develop as critical thinkers is to nurture competent use of five types of tools of thinking. These categories of tools are *background knowledge, criteria for judgment, critical thinking vocabulary, thinking strategies* and *habits of mind.* The chart on the next page offers a sampling of the tools for thinking critically in history.

Assessing for the tools

Assessment is an important complement to the teaching of the tools of critical thinking. As suggested by the familiar adages "What is counted counts" and "Testing drives the curriculum," evaluation has important implications for what students consider important and ultimately what students learn. Evaluations that focus exclusively on recall of information or never consider habits of mind fail to assess, and possibly discourage, student growth in critical reflection.

A key challenge in assessing critical thinking is deciding what to look for in a student's answer. If there is no single correct response, we may well ask: "On what basis, then, can we reliably assess students?" In the case of critical thinking, we would want to see how well students exhibited the qualities of a competent thinker. Thus, the intellectual resources or tools for critical thinking in history become the criteria for assessing students' work. The example on page 78 suggests each of the five types of critical thinking tools and specific assessment criteria that might be considered when evaluating critical thinking in an argumentative essay in history.

Background Knowledge
—the information about a topic required for thoughtful reflection

Students cannot think deeply about a topic if they know little about it. Three questions to ask in developing this tool:

- What do students need to know about the events in the historical period?
- What do students need to know about the prevailing conditions and norms?
- What information would be helpful to know about the topic or phenomenon (e.g., race relations, warfare)?

Criteria for Judgment
—the considerations or grounds for deciding which of the alternatives is the most sensible or appropriate

Critical thinking is essentially a matter of judging which alternative is sensible or reasonable. Students need help in thinking carefully about the criteria to use when judging various alternatives.

- Is the information *accurate*?
- Is the interpretation *plausible?*
- Is the conclusion *justifiable*?
- Is the event *significant*?

Critical Thinking Vocabulary
—the range of concepts and distinctions that are helpful when thinking critically

Students require the vocabulary or concepts that permit them to make important distinctions among the different issues and thinking tasks facing them. These include the following:

- cause and consequence;
- historical perspective versus presentism;
- primary and secondary source;
- bias and point of view.

Thinking Strategies
—the repertoire of heuristics, organizing devices, models and algorithms that may be useful when thinking through a critical thinking problem

Although critical thinking is never simply a matter of following certain procedures or steps, numerous strategies are useful for guiding one's performance when thinking critically:

- *Making decisions:* Are there models or procedures to guide students through the factors they should consider (e.g., a framework for issue analysis or problem solving)?
- *Organizing information:* Would a graphic organizer (e.g., webbing diagrams, Venn diagrams, "pro and con" charts) be useful in representing what a student knows about the issue?
- *Role taking:* Before deciding on an action that affects others, should students put themselves in the others' positions and imagine their feelings?

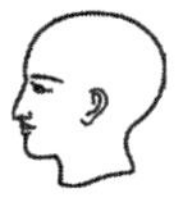

Habits of Mind
—the values and attitudes of a careful and conscientious thinker

Being able to apply criteria and use strategies is of little value unless students also have the habits of mind of a thoughtful person. These include:

- *Open-minded:* Are students willing to consider evidence opposing their view and to revise their view should the evidence warrant it?
- *Fair-minded:* Are students willing to give impartial consideration to alternative points of view and not simply impose their preference?
- *Independent-minded:* Are students willing to stand up for their firmly held beliefs?
- *Inquiring or "critical" attitude:* Are students inclined to question the clarity of and support for claims and to seek justified beliefs and values?

Type of criteria for assessment	Evidence of critical thinking in a persuasive way
Background knowledge	• cited accurate information • understood the key facts
Criteria for judgment	• provided ample evidence • arranged arguments in logical sequence
Critical thinking vocabulary	• correctly distinguished "arguments" from "counter arguments" • understood what is implied by historical perspective
Thinking strategies	• used appropriate strategies for persuasive writing
Habits of mind	• demonstrated an openness to alternative perspectives • refrained from forming firm opinions where the evidence was inconclusive

Blackline Masters

10

Comparing significance

	Event:	Event:	Event:
Prominence at the time *Immediate recognition:* Was it noticed at the time as having importance? *Duration:* How long did it exist or operate?			
Consequences *Magnitude of impact:* How deeply felt or profound was its impact? *Scope of impact:* How widespread was it impact? *Lasting nature of impact:* How long-lasting were its effects?			
Subsequent profile *Remembered:* Has it been memorialized? *Revealing:* Does it inform our understanding of a historical issue? (Is it emblematic of a condition or period?)			

Ranking	Event	Explanation
1st		
2nd		
3rd		

Analyzing traces

	Evidence	Conclusions
Who *Who is in the image?* *Who would use the object?*		
What *What are the people in the image doing?* *What is the object?*		
Where *Where does the action take place?* *Where would the object be used?*		
When *When does the action take place?* *When would the object be used?*		
Why *Why are they doing this action?* *Why would the object be used—what is its function?*		
How *How did the people come to be in this situation?* *How was the object created and used?*		

What questions about the past might this source help us answer?	What answers can we draw from this source about these questions?	What evidence can we offer to support our answers?

Judging the credibility of primary accounts

	Relevant information	Conclusions about credibility
Full accounting: How faithful to the events and complete is the account? How do we know?		
General qualifications: How qualified is the author to report on the event?		
Access to information: Was the author in a well-informed position to observe or experience the event?		
Conflict of interest: Is there a conflict of interest that might prejudice the account?		
Social perspective: How will the author's social situation and beliefs influence the account?		
Internal consistency: Is there consistency in the facts within the account?		
Consistency with other information: Does the account align with or contradict other accounts?		
Believability: Does the account seem plausible?		

Overall conclusion

❑ Highly credible ❑ Probably credible ❑ Questionable ❑ Not at all credible

Explanation

Assessing secondary accounts

	Strengths regarding justifiability	Questions and concerns about justifiability
Dependable sources: Do the sources of information seem reliable? Is there reason to suspect their authenticity or credibility?		
Relevant facts: Does the information relate to the argument for which it is being used?		
Adequate evidence. Is there enough evidence to support the conclusions offered by the historian?		
Conflicting evidence. Is there evidence to support different conclusions than the ones presented in the account?		

Summary conclusion

❑ Very strongly justified ❑ Partially justified ❑ Questionable ❑ Very weakly justified

Explanation

Using multiple historical sources

The following are guidelines for arriving at and defending a conclusion using multiple primary and secondary sources.

Type of source: Identify whether each is a primary or secondary source.

Summary of ideas: Paraphrase or list in point form what is actually reported in each document.

Authorship: Consider who authored or created each document and what is know about the person or group. How might this affect the information presented?

Context: Try to identify a purpose and intended audience for each document. Consider how this might affect credibility.

Inferences: Look to draw inferences from each source about the question you are trying to answer?

Corroboration: Check if any of the sources support or challenge the inferences drawn.

Conclusion: Considering all of the evidence, offer a conclusion that clearly and specifically answers the question offered for consideration.

Justification: Support your conclusion with evidence from the sources and suggest why alternative hypotheses are not as plausible as the conclusion you are putting forward. If applicable, explain why sources which may seem to contradict your conclusion are not really a concern.

Document analysis

Document	Source (primary or secondary), authorship and context	Possible relevance	Summary of key points	Inferences about the question under consideration

Then and now

What do I know? Here are **100** questions to find out what was Canada like exactly **200** years ago. Working individually or with a partner, indicate your answer in the box whether each item was present at the time: **Yes** it was, **No** it wasn't, or **Don't Know.**

1. cars
2. large cities
3. houses
4. apartments
5. schools from grades K-12
6. universities
7. scholarships
8. blue jeans
9. jean shorts
10. button up jeans
11. high heel shoes
12. running shoes
13. t-shirts
14. ties
15. earrings
16. reading glasses
17. felt pens
18. sandals
19. women's two piece bathing suits
20. CD players
21. lip stick
22. radios
23. bicycles
24. motorbikes
25. working hours from 9:00-5:00
26. daylight savings
27. perfumes
28. deodorants
29. belts to hold up pants
30. umbrellas
31. summer holidays
32. hospitals
33. hand watches
34. roads from Montreal to Vancouver
35. war in North America
36. Olympics
37. cameras
38. sailboats
39. trains
40. planes
41. newspapers
42. magazines for teenagers
43. professional sports teams
44. after-school sports teams
45. sunglasses
46. theaters
47. televisions
48. e-mail
49. doctors
50. lawyers
51. mail delivery
52. farmers
53. bankers
54. accountants
55. golfers
56. musicians
57. taxis
58. record players
59. canoes
60. government campgrounds
61. rifles
62. spears
63. guns
64. Interact (ATM) banking
65. churches
66. mosques
67. Canadians
68. people in British Columbia
69. Coke or Pepsi
70. elected politicians
71. coffee
72. ice cream cones
73. movie theatres
74. beer
75. restaurants
76. dating
77. buttons on clothes
78. zippers
79. libraries
80. baseball caps worn by teenagers
81. toilets
82. showers
83. hair dressers
84. sunscreen
85. candy bars
86. plastic bags
87. tennis courts
88. telephones
89. police officers
90. mayors of cities
91. cereal boxes
92. shopping malls
93. refrigerators
94. stoves
95. calculators
96. vitamin pills
97. candles
98. electricity
99. gum
100. wallets

Web of effects

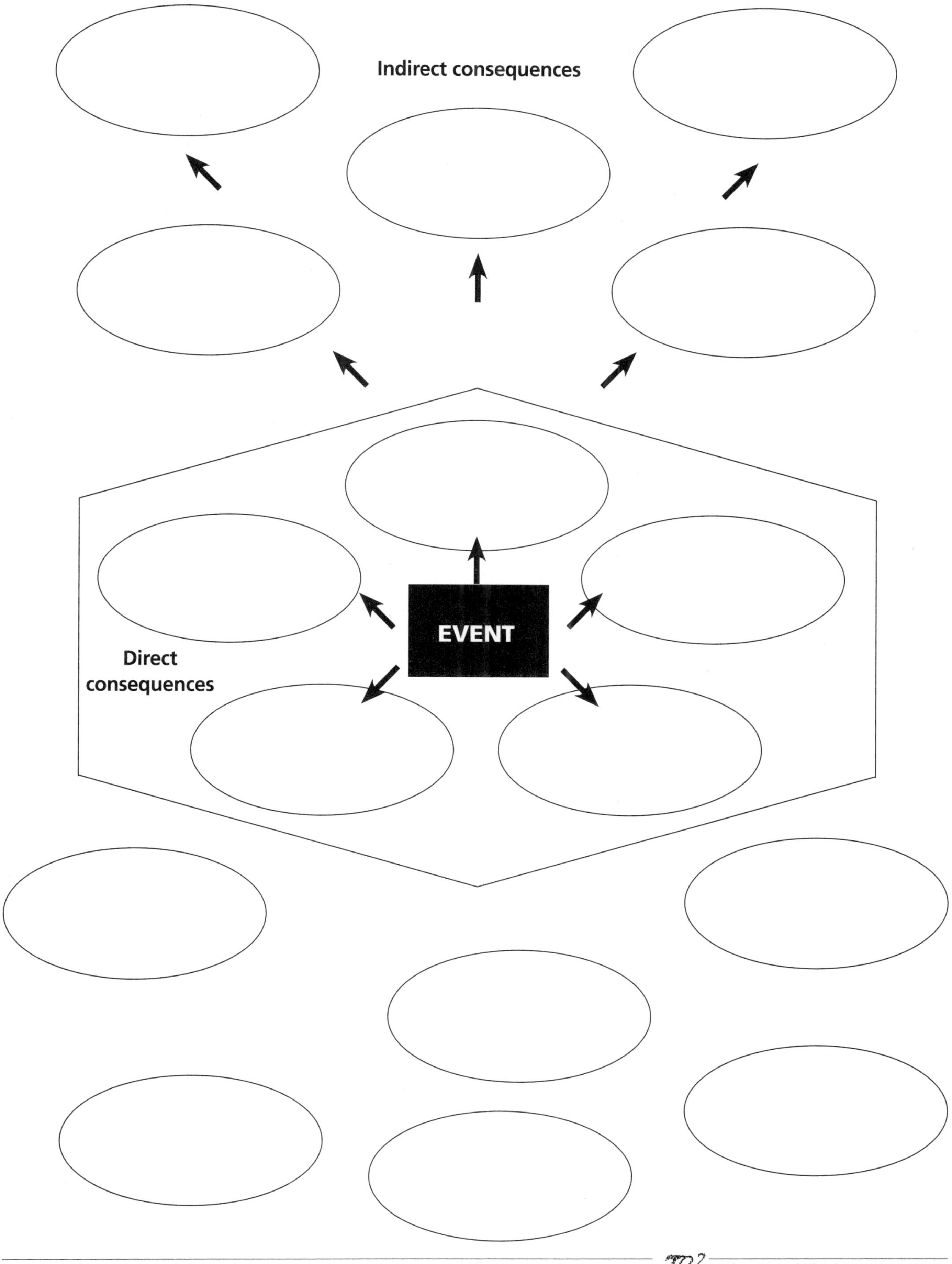

Impact assessment report

Assess the economic, social and political consequences of the assigned event on the identified individual or group. Assess their wellbeing using the grading scale provided. In the bottom half, provide specific evidence explaining the consequences for each group.

Individual or group

	1.	2.	3.	4.	Grading scale
Economic					A Excellent B Very good C+ Good C Adequate C– Poor D Very poor F Failing
Social					
Political					
Overall average					

Explanation of impact on each individual's/group's wellbeing			
1.	2.	3.	4.

Historical profile

Indicate on the scales your assigned historical character's attitude on each issue. Provide two supporting reasons for each rating.

Assigned role: ______________________________

	5	4	3	2	1
Loyalty to Canada	**5**	**4**	**3**	**2**	**1**
	strongly patriotic				strongly unpatriotic

Rationale

-
-

Views on immigration	**5**	**4**	**3**	**2**	**1**
	highly selective				very welcoming

Rationale

-
-

Cultural perspective	**5**	**4**	**3**	**2**	**1**
	single dominant culture				strong multiculturalist

Rationale

-
-

Economic orientation	**5**	**4**	**3**	**2**	**1**
	strongly capitalist				strongly socialist

Rationale

-
-

Simon Fraser descending the Fraser River, 1808

From the Imperial Oil Collection

Map of the Fraser River

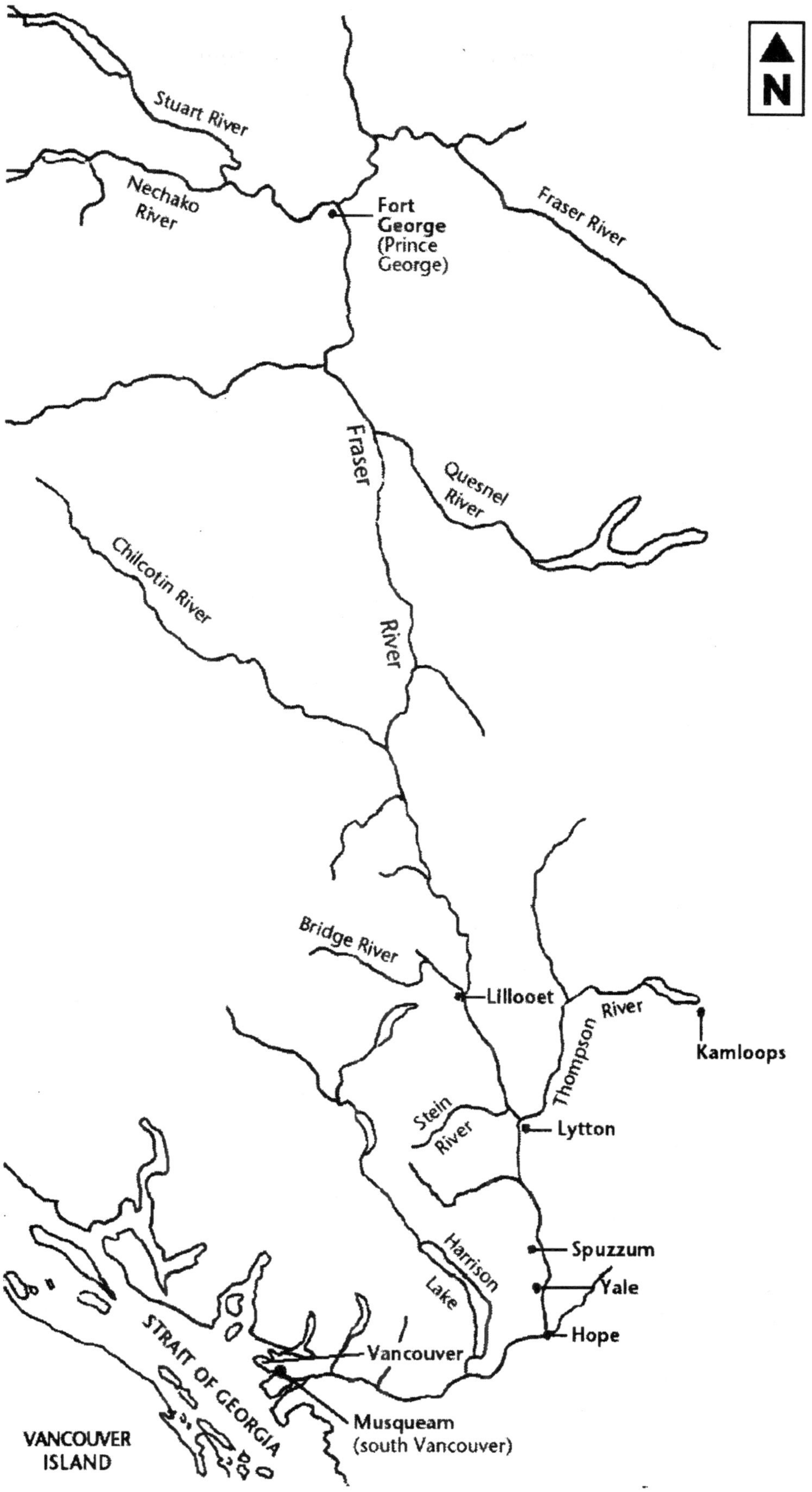

Assessing the rankings

	Well developed	Competent	Underdeveloped
Identifies relevant evidence	Identifies the key pieces of evidence for each criterion.	Identifies obvious pieces of evidence for each criterion, but overlooks some important considerations.	Identifies very little evidence for each criterion.
Justifies rankings	Justification for each ranking shows thoughtful consideration of the most important factors.	Justification for each ranking touches upon some key factors.	No plausible justification is given for any of the assigned rankings.

Comments:

Fraser's journey[1]

In the early morning of May 28, 1808 Simon Fraser with twenty-three men in four canoes left Fort George. His instructions from his superiors at the North West Company were to find a route from the interior of British Columbia to the Pacific Ocean along the river which Fraser imagined to be the Columbia River. Day after day they encountered obstacles as they paddled down the river. The river was a continuous series of rapids and the carrying places were extremely dangerous or very long. The places where they had to carry their canoes to get around the rapids were so rough that a pair of moccasins was worn to shreds in one day. Fraser decided the Indians he had met were correct in saying that the river was not passable for canoes. On June 10, they built a scaffold to store their canoes and buried the equipment they could not carry with them. Fraser and his men set out on foot, carrying packs weighing eighty pounds each. In his diary, Fraser wrote that they experienced "a good deal of fatigue and disagreeable walking" but he and his men continued on their journey.

Soon they met Indians who told them ten more days would bring them to the sea. One villager said that he had been to the sea and had seen "great canoes" and white men. When Fraser and his party proceeded, many of the locals walked with them. Two days later, at a large village (near present day Lillooet), Indians told them that the river was navigable from their village to the sea, whereupon Fraser bargained for two canoes. At another village (now Lytton) the people were so friendly that Fraser was called upon to shake hands with twelve hundred of them. In return he and his men were well fed and were able to get two additional canoes.

Despite what the Indians had said about the river being navigable, the explorers soon found their way blocked by numerous rapids. Two canoes were lost. More canoes were obtained from the natives. During this time, the explorers toiled over the roughest country they had ever seen:

> *We had to pass over huge rocks assisted by the Indians . . . As for the road by land, we could scarcely make our way with even only our guns. I have been for a long period among the Rocky Mountains, but have never seen any thing like this country. It is so wild that I cannot find words to describe our situation at times. We had to pass where no human being should venture; yet in those places there is a regular footpath impressed, or rather indented upon the very rocks by frequent travelling. Besides this, steps which are formed like a ladder . . . furnish a safe and convenient passage to the Natives; but we, who had not the advantage of their education and experience, were often in imminent danger when obliged to follow their example.* [extract from Fraser's Journal]

At Spuzzum, Fraser was much impressed by a number of totem poles, each fifteen feet high and "carved in a curious but rude manner, yet pretty well proportioned". Friendly Indians living in large frame houses presented them with roast salmon. Near where the town of Hope now stands, they were entertained at a large village where there was a huge community house built of cedar planks. Some Indians warned that the natives of the coast were "wicked" and would attack them, but Fraser would not alter his plan. When these Indians refused to lend him a canoe Fraser took one by force. For a short while canoes from the village followed them, their occupants waving weapons and shouting war songs, but Fraser and his men ignored them. Soon after, another group came at them "howling like wolves" and swinging war clubs, but they did not attack Fraser's group. Fraser ordered his men to paddle farther along to a second village, but the behaviour of the Indians forced them to turn back. On July 2, near what is now New Westminster, Fraser decided to return up the river in order to secure provisions before attempting to resume his descent to the ocean. This was the farthest distance reached by the explorers. Fraser's reception by the natives he encountered on his return up the river was far from friendly—one group seized a canoe and began to pillage the baggage. Fraser forced a canoe from them and left a blanket in return. For several days hostile Indians followed them. They finally reached friendly villages and were guided over rough bridges and swaying ladders by natives who "went up and down these wild places with the same agility as sailors do on board a ship".

Fraser finally arrived back at Fort George on August 6. Although Fraser had not accomplished his purpose of exploring the Columbia River, his voyage did clear up the confusion between the Fraser River and Columbia River that existed among European fur traders.

---

[1] Adapted from M. G. Parks. Undated. "The descent of the Fraser River" in *Discoverers and Explorers in Canada—1763-1911* (Portfolio II #4), illustrated by Charles W. Jefferys and published by Imperial Oil Ltd.

Looking for significance

Describe six events and explain their significance in light of the following factors:

- *Was prominent at the time* (Was it a noticeable event then?)
- *Had notable consequences* (Did it affect the rest of the trip and beyond the trip?)
- *Determined subsequent profile* (Is it memorable or revealing about Fraser?)

Summary of incident	Possible significance

Selections from Fraser's diary

The following are a few of the entries in the diary that Fraser kept as he travelled the Fraser River.[1]

May 28, 1808

Having made every necessary preparation for a long voyage, we embarked at 5 o'clock A.M. in four canoes at Fraser's River [probably the Nechaco River]. Our crew consisted of nineteen men, two Indians, Mr. Stuart, Mr. Quesnel and myself, in all twenty-four.

May 30, 1808

These Indians have heard of fire-arms, but had never seen any, and they evinced [showed] a great desire of seeing ours and obtaining explanations as to their use. In compliance, we fired several shots whose reports astonished them so as to make them drop off their legs. Upon recovering from their surprise, we made them examine their effect. They appeared quite uneasy on seeing the marks on the trees and observed that the Indians in that quarter [local region] were good and peaceable, and would never make use of their arms to annoy white people; yet they remarked that we ought to be on our guard, and proceed with great care when approaching villages, for, should we surprise the Natives, they might take us as enemies, and, through fear, attack us with their arrows.

May 31, 1808

The Chief and the Indians recommended to our attention yesterday and who were encamped on a hill to the left, soon joined us and presented us with dried salmon and different kinds of roots; the last, we could not well relish [like the taste], though highly recommended by them. After enquiring repeatedly for the slave who had a knowledge of the country below, he was at last introduced. To form an estimate of his capacity, I had two oil cloths spread out for the ground of a chart upon which I desired him to sketch the country towards the sea. . . . We could however plainly see in his sketch a confirmation of what had been told us of the difficulties of the navigation and, thereby, the necessity of leaving our canoes, with as much of our baggage as we could spare, in order to continue our journey by land.

June 1, 1808

Numbers of the Natives came to see us in the course of the day and remained. They assured us that the navigation for a certain distance below was impracticable, and advised us to leave our canoes in their charge and proceed on our journey by land to a great river that flows from the left into this communication. The country they said consisted of plains, and the journey could be performed with horses in four or five days; thence we should have smooth water all the way to the sea. But going to the sea by an indirect way was not the object of the undertaking. I therefore would not deviate and continued our route according to my original intention.

June 3, 1808

. . . Last night a 4th Indian, who seemed to be well acquainted with the river, promised to accompany us, but this morning declined, saying he was afraid of the rapids; another brought us a pistol which Mr. Quesnel lost yesterday while on horseback; this was a piece of honesty we hardly expected, though, I must say, that during the whole time we were there, and although many things were let loose and scattered about us in such a manner as to afford all opportunity to the Natives, nothing went astray . . .

June 9, 1808

The Indians of this place drew a chart of the river below which represented it to us as a dreadful chain of apparently insurmountable difficulties; at the same time they blamed us for venturing so far with our canoes and for not passing by land, as advised by the old chief of a former occasion, asserting that this communication [the Fraser River], both by land and by water, would in some places be found impracticable to strangers, as we should have to ascend and descend mountains and precipices [cliffs] by means of rope ladders, &c.

June 13, 1808

This morning, lost some time mending our shoes. We fired several shots to show the Natives the effects of our guns, and set out at five accompanied by all the Natives with two horses; three more horsemen soon joined our party. Having halted, one of the strangers took our interpreter's gun through curiosity, and, while examining it, touched the trigger; one of our men having observed him in time, threw up the muzzle as the shot was going off and thus saved the lives of some Natives who otherwise would have received the contents; such misfortune would have at once put an end to our journey

1 From L.R. Masson. 1889. *Les bougeois de la Compagnie du Nord-Ouest,* Quebec: A Coté et Cie, Volume 1 pp. 157-221.

and perhaps to our lives. When we came to the Forks (of the Lilloet and Fraser) the Chief men, dressed in their coats of mail, advanced to meet us in order to know our dispositions [character and intentions] before we could be admitted into their camp. Our Chief harangued [gave a speech to] them in his own language; they answered him in theirs, and we were obliged to employ three interpreters on the occasion to settle the affair. These ambassadors are of the Askettih nation; they looked manly and had really the appearance of warriors. They seemed to speak with a fluency which attracted a kind of attention indicative of applause, and our Chief conveyed our sentiments and wishes with great animation. He assured the Askettih nation that we were good people and had nothing to do with the quarrels of Indian nations. Here we became acquainted with a man of the Chilkcotin tribe who had left his own country when a boy, . . . He observed that he had been to the sea by this communication, where he had seen men like us who lived in a wooden enclosure [fort] upon an island, . . . He gave us a good account of the navigation and consented to accompany us as pilot. Since the departure of our Tha-how-tin interpreter, this was the only man with whom we could converse to any advantage. Continued our course with a strong current for about nine miles where the river expands into a lake. Here we saw seals and a large river coming from the left and a round mountain ahead which the Natives called Stremotch [Mount Baker]. After sunset, we encamped upon the right side of the river. At this place, the trees were remarkably large, cedars five fathoms [thirty feet] in circumference and proportionate height. Musquitoes were in clouds. We had nothing to eat; the Natives, who always gave us plenty of provisions in their villages, were all as destitute [in great need] as ourselves. Though at a great distance from home, they carried no arms about them, from which we inferred that they had full confidence either in our goodness or in their numbers.

July 10, 1808

The Indians certainly deserve our grateful remembrance for their able assistance throughout these alarming situations. The descents were, if possible, still more difficult; in these places, we were under the necessity of trusting our things to the Indians, even our guns were handed from one to another, yet they thought nothing of it, they went up and down these wild places with the same agility as sailors do on board a ship. After escaping innumerable perils in the course of the day, we encamped about sunset; the Indians tried to fish but caught nothing; they however supplied us with plenty of dried fish.

July 11, 1808

Started early accompanied by many Indians as usual. Previous to our departure the Chief gave us forty salmons and sent young men along with us to carry them saying: "The Indians above are poor"; I returned the chief's compliment to his satisfaction. We could not procure [obtain] canoes, the Indians said the rapids were too strong to make use of them to any advantage. Soon after we had left the camp, the Indian who had supplied us with a canoe going down joined our party and offered his services again in like manner, which we accepted and found useful for many purposes in course of the day. We passed the village where the Indians were so poor according to the account of the chief, yet they generously shared with us what little they had . . .

July 20, 1808

Early in the morning, we proceeded on our journey and soon after joined Mr. Stuart, when we had the inexpressible satisfaction of finding our canoes and our cache [hidden supplies] perfectly safe. For this good fortune we felt grateful to the Indians who continually attended to their security during our absence . . .

July 22, 1808

At 8 A.M., we arrived at the rapide couvert [covered rapids] which is more than a mile long and where we were obliged to carry all our baggage over long and steep hills; here we found Indians among whom were the old Atnah chief and his brother both so overjoyed to see us that they annoyed us with caresses [hugs]. They assured us that they felt extremely anxious for our safety during our absence, and that they had determined, if the Indians of the sea destroyed us, to collect their friends and go to revenge us . . .

Quesnel's account of the trip[1]

Now I must tell you that I went exploring this summer with Mr. Simon Fraser and John Stuart, whom I believe you know. We were accompanied by 12 men in three canoes. Went down the river that up until now was thought to be the Columbia but finding it very soon unnavigable, we left our canoes and continued our journey on foot in the most appalling mountain that we could never have crossed if the natives, who received us well, had not helped us. After having passed all these difficult spots, not without much trouble as you can imagine, we found the river once more navigable and all embarked in wooden canoes and continued on our way more comfortably, as far as the place where the river empties into the Pacific Ocean. We were well treated by all the other Indians on our return trip and all arrived in excellent health in our New Caledonia. The mouth of the river is in Latitude 49°, nearly three degrees north of the real Columbia. This journey did not meet the needs of the Company and will never be of any advantage to them, this river not being navigable, but we have nothing to reproach ourselves with, having done what we set out to do.

[1] From a letter by Jules Quesnel, one of Fraser's two lieutenants on the trip.

A twentieth century account[1]

On May 22 Fraser and eight men left Fort Fraser to ride the Columbia to its mouth. It was a voyage to curl a man's hair and in his portrait, Fraser's hair does appear somewhat curly. They were rolled and buffetted by vicious rapids. At one point the river look so bad they climbed the canyon wall on stone steps cut into the rock face by the Indians, and crept along the track at the top of the canyon. Able to return to the waterway at a point of relative calm, they reached the delta on July 2, worn and shaken by their experience, only to be chased for six miles across the water by hostile Indians.

Simon Fraser was dismayed and disgusted by the Columbia. It was obviously useless for freight canoes and the country was too hot and dry for furs. Fraser had decided that the Columbia was the worst river he'd ever seen, when he made an important discovery. He surveyed his position and found it wasn't the Columbia at all. The Columbia entered the ocean below the 47th parallel and he was north of the 49th. Simon called his discovery the Bad River, one of the nicer names he could think of. His friend, David Thompson, later named it the Fraser and Fraser responded by naming a river he had discovered in honour of Thompson.

[1] From T. Cashman. 1971. *An illustrated history of Western Canada*. Edmonton, AB: M.G. Hurtig.

Revising the account

Proposed conclusion about Fraser's journey ______________________________

Additions or changes to the account	Evidence to support recommendations

Before and after profiles

Character traits (start)	Supporting evidence

Character traits (end)	Supporting evidence

Assessing character traits

	Exemplary	Good	Satisfactory	Remedial
Revealing character traits	Overall, the identified traits reveal key aspects of the historical character.	The identified traits reveal many key aspects but a few important aspects are ignored or incorrectly identified.	Some of the identified traits reveal key aspects of the historical character.	Almost all the identified traits reflect trivial or mistaken aspects of the historical character.
Plausible explanations for identified traits	All the explanations offer highly credible, clear reasons why the identified traits are plausible.	Most explanations offer credible and clear reasons why the identified traits are plausible.	Some of the explanations offer credible and clear reasons why the identified traits are plausible.	No credible and clear reasons are offered why the identified traits are plausible.

Comments:

Justifying my conclusion

I believe he had

- ❑ changed greatly
- ❑ changed quite a bit
- ❑ changed in a few respects
- ❑ hardly changed at all

The main reasons in support of my conclusion are

-
-
-
-

The best reasons why others might disagree with my conclusions are

-
-
-
-

I think my conclusion is more reasonable because

-
-

Assessing the justification

	Well developed	Competent	Underdeveloped
Reasons for conclusion	Clearly describes important reasons for the chosen conclusion.	Identifies some relevant reasons for the chosen conclusion.	Provides no relevant reasons for the chosen conclusion.
Reasons for alternative conclusions	Clearly describes the important reasons to support other conclusions.	Identifies some relevant reasons to support other conclusions.	Identifies no relevant reasons reasons to support other conclusions.
Justification for preferred conclusion	Offers a thoughtful justification why the selected conclusion is more reasonable.	Offers some justification why the selected conclusion is more reasonable.	Offers no justification why the selected conclusion is more reasonable.

Comments:

Explaining their actions

Incident #1: ____

Possible explanation	Evidence

Incident #2: ____

Possible explanation	Evidence

Incident #3: ____

Possible explanation	Evidence

A First Nations account[1]

"I was there when Simon Fraser came. All the people were frightened . . . It was seen that some of the people in the canoes were just like those who had come in the white-winged canoes . . . The faces of some were pale; others had big beards. They wore strange clothes.

We looked at them closely, and saw that the eyes of some of them were blue like the sky, and others grey like the clouds. Yes, they must be sky people . . . We touched their clothes. They were strange; not like blankets made from dogs' hair, or from skins or cedar bark . . .

Whattlekainum, one of the sub-chiefs, tried to talk to them, but they had strange tongues . . . The chief of the Sky-people (Fraser) made signs (that) he was on his way to the sea . . .

When the canoe of the chief started down the river, one of the men took what looked like a crane, and put the legs over his shoulder and blew on the head of it, and made his fingers dance on the bird's bill—and strange sounds were made . . . The noise went up the river and back . . .

The next day they came back to Kikait and they all came ashore. Some of them took out small sticks with knobs on them and put them in their mouths. Then they took out bags and made fire, and put it on the end of the sticks and smoke came out of their mouths. We thought they would burn up, but this did not happen, so we knew they were supernatural.

Then the chief of the Sky-people showed us what we thought was a big stick. He cut and peeled some small willows and put them up, crossed, one over the other. Then he went back some distance and pointed the big stick at the twigs. We nearly died, for fire came from the big stick and made thunder, and the smaller sticks fell over.

The strangers stayed all night . . . In the morning some things were missing (from their canoes). The white chief became angry. Some of his men searched among the people and found the articles our young men had taken. They took the things from the young men and kicked them. That was bad . . . It is (not) right to kick a warrior. It makes them ashamed. So the hearts of the young men grew black within them . . . They got ready to follow and kill them.

---

[1] Excerpt from B. McKelvie. 1947. *Fort Langley.*

Self-assessment of discussion

	Exemplary	Good	Satisfactory	Developing	Remedial
Background knowledge – *accurate use of relevant facts*	I am able to refer to many relevant facts, always with accuracy	I am able to refer to relevant facts, most often with accuracy	I am able to refer to relevant facts, usually with accuracy	I am able to refer to a limited number of relevants facts with little accuracy	I am able to refer to few or no relevant and accurate facts
Open-mindedness – *open to consider a variety of views* – *willing to re-think position based on new evidence or arguments*	I always carefully consider all viewpoints presented I am always willing to reconsider my position when evidence or arguments warrant	I usually consider most viewpoints presented I am usually willing to reconsider my position when evidence or arguments warrant	I occasionally consider a variety of viewpoints presented I am sometimes willing to reconsider my position when evidence or arguments warrant	I seldom consider other viewpoints I am rarely willing to reconsider my position when evidence or arguments warrant	I rarely or never consider other view-points I am always reluctant to reconsider my position when evidence or arguments warrant
Reasoned judgment – *uses evidence to reach an informed decision* – *considers criteria when making a decision*	My decisions are always based on available evidence I always consider the range of criteria when arriving at a decision	My decisions are usually based on available evidence I usually consider most of the criteria when arriving at a decision	My decisions are some-times based on avail-able evidence I sometimes consider criteria when arriving at a decision	My decisions are seldom based on available evidence I seldom consider criteria when arriving at a decision	My decisions are rarely based on available evidence I rarely or never con-sider criteria when arriving at a decision

Comments: